Cinematic Overtures

Leonard Hastings Schoff Memorial Lectures

University Seminars
Leonard Hastings Schoff Memorial Lectures

The University Seminars at Columbia University sponsor an annual series of lectures, with the support of the Leonard Hastings Schoff and Suzanne Levick Schoff Memorial Fund. A member of the Columbia faculty is invited to deliver before a general audience three lectures on a topic of his or her choosing. Columbia University Press publishes the lectures.

Charles Larmore, *The Romantic Legacy* 1996

Saskia Sassen, *Losing Control? Sovereignty in the Age of Globalization* 1996

David Cannadine, *The Rise and Fall of Class in Britain* 1999

Ira Katznelson, *Desolation and Enlightenment: Political Knowledge After Total War, Totalitarianism, and the Holocaust* 2003

Lisa Anderson, *Pursuing Truth, Exercising Power: Social Science and Public Policy in the Twenty-First Century* 2003

Partha Chatterjee, *The Politics of the Governed: Reflections on Popular Politics in Most of the World* 2004

David Rosand, *The Invention of Painting in America* 2004

George Rupp, *Globalization Challenged: Conviction, Conflict, Community* 2006

Lesley A. Sharp, *Bodies, Commodities, and Biotechnologies: Death, Mourning, and Scientific Desire in the Realm of Human Organ Transfer* 2007

Robert W. Hanning, *Serious Play: Desire and Authority in the Poetry of Ovid, Chaucer, and Ariosto* 2010

Boris Gasparov, *Beyond Pure Reason: Ferdinand de Saussure's Philosophy of Language and Its Early Romantic Antecedents* 2012

Douglas A. Chalmers, *Reforming Democracies: Six Facts About Politics That Demand a New Agenda* 2013

Philip Kitcher, *Deaths in Venice: The Cases of Gustav von Aschenbach* 2013

Robert L. Belknap, *Plots* 2016

Paige West, *Dispossession and the Environment: Rhetoric and Inequality in Papua New Guinea* 2016

Cinematic Overtures

HOW TO READ OPENING SCENES

Annette Insdorf

Columbia University Press
New York

Columbia University Press
Publishers Since 1893
New York   Chichester, West Sussex
cup.columbia.edu

Library of Congress Cataloging-in-Publication Data
Names: Insdorf, Annette, author.
Title: Cinematic overtures : how to read opening scenes /
Annette Insdorf.
Description: New York : Columbia University Press, [2017] |
Series: Leonard Hastings Schoff memorial lectures | Includes
bibliographical references and index.
Identifiers: LCCN 2017009183 | ISBN 9780231182249
(cloth : alk. paper) | ISBN 9780231182256 (pbk. : alk. paper) |
ISBN 9780231544061 (e-book)
Subjects: LCSH: Motion pictures.
Classification: LCC PN1994 .I4645 2017 | DDC 791.43—dc23
LC record available at https://lccn.loc.gov/2017009183

Printed in the United States of America

Cover image: Film still from *The Piano*. Image provided by
the author with permission from Jane Campion,
the film's writer and director.

Cover design: Lisa Hamm

Dedicated to the memory of Guy Gallo

Contents

Preface

First impressions count. A strong opening sequence leads the spectator to trust the filmmakers. My experience watching films—as well as teaching cinema history and criticism—suggests that a great movie tends to provide in the first few minutes the keys by which to unlock the rest of the film. Gifted directors know how to layer the first shots in a way that prepares for their thematic concerns and stylistic approach. Sometimes the opening sequence is intentionally misleading, inviting the viewer into active participation with the film, alert to the images and sounds that will be developed throughout subsequent scenes.

This book initially took shape as a series of lectures I was invited to deliver at Columbia University. In November 2014 I offered three Leonard Hastings Schoff Memorial Lectures— "Opening as Prologue," "Opening as Misdirection," and "Opening as Action"—including numerous film clips. Reshaping the lectures into a book meant finding a new and more coherent structure, which led to these eight distinct approaches to opening a motion picture. Because adaptation places cinematic storytelling in relief, I also highlight three case studies of a striking opening translated from a novel.

If *Cinematic Overtures* had been conceived as strictly a book of film analysis for other scholars or students, I would not be using the first person singular. But since I hope the book will reach a diverse group of readers interested in thinking and talking about film, the "I"—and all the idiosyncratic connections it implies—remains. Each section is designed as a first step—rather than end point—to engender the reader's heightened viewing of films and reflection upon them. The tone is purposefully accessible, intended to reach a wide audience of cinephiles both within and outside academia. As the title proposes, the reader is invited to enter into the unfolding of meaning through close analysis of opening sequences. To provide a visual reference for this written text, I have included frame enlargements. (The electronic version of the book has an accompanying compendium of carefully selected clips.)

High-profile titles and undiscovered gems rub shoulders throughout *Cinematic Overtures*. This mix of mainstream and high-art films reflects my own overlapping areas of scholarship and journalism. I have included lesser-known motion pictures—often with more detailed analysis than the famous ones—in the hope that readers will seek them out. While it might be unusual for an author to cite her students' papers, teaching at Columbia nurtures a book of this kind: the essays of both MFA and undergraduate students often reveal how sophisticated films engage viewers and generate insights. I believe that all of the titles discussed here are linked by the alertness and engagement they ask of viewers from the very beginning. Although we often watch movies without looking attentively or hear without listening closely, through openings like those described in *Cinematic Overtures*, filmmakers trust the audience to actively make connections.

I appreciate the wise counsel of Philip Leventhal, my editor at Columbia University Press, and the ongoing support of my agent, Georges Borchardt. For the invitation to deliver the Schoff Lectures at Columbia, I am grateful to Robert Pollack. Robert Brink, my digital editor, provided valuable assistance with frame enlargements and clip selection. Finally, I thank Mark Ethan Toporek for viewing films with me, suggesting areas of exploration, reading drafts with a constructively critical eye, and being the most loving ally.

Cinematic Overtures

1

The Crafted Frame

Saul Bass, *Talk to Her, Knife in the Water, Camouflage*

My point of departure is close analysis of the opening sequences of motion pictures. When discussing films, I share with other viewers how superior movies provide within the first few minutes the thematic and stylistic components that will be developed throughout the film. This is of course similar to how great novels offer in the initial two paragraphs the keys by which to unlock the rest of the book. In addition to establishing the tone—whether tense, ironic, romantic, frightening, comic, nostalgic, or self-conscious—the opening introduces meaningful motifs; these can include windows, circular images, or elemental imagery such as water and earth. The opening makes us aware of the point of view: who is telling the story. Once upon a time, "once upon a time" were the four words that introduced a tale. The voice of the omniscient third-person narrator framed the story with a soothing movement into a past. Film is also "once upon a *space*"—or, more appropriately, "once *into* a *space*"—as the camera explores the space of the frame. *Psycho* and *Sunset Boulevard* provide fine examples, moving voyeuristically from an exterior "objective" shot into a window, penetrating a room's intimacy.

Why focus on the instigating moments of a motion picture? Victor Hugo called opening signals "inexorable revealers."[1] This quotation appears in an excellent article by Victor Brombert; while his essay "Opening Signals in Narrative" refers to the beginning of literary texts, his description is fruitfully applicable to cinematic ones. And I share Brombert's appreciation of Maurice Merleau-Ponty when he ascribes the following assumption to this philosopher: "That the choice of every artistic technique ultimately corresponded to a metaphysical perspective. Indeed, all narrative structures, because of the notion of a beginning and an ending, necessarily set up a tension between linear and cyclical structures. And the specific nature of this tension in any given work also engages a conceptual, moral, or philosophical debate."[2]

My chapter divisions—much like my Schoff Lecture titles—are not rigid but fluid and overlapping. An opening can be both a prelude and a misleading introduction (for example, when the voice-over narration is spoken by a character who turns out be dead). And an opening can be part of the action while providing the equivalent of a frame around a painting. Philip Kaufman's *Quills* (2000) is a vibrant illustration, opening with the image of a beautiful young woman as the male voice-over says, "Dear Reader, I've a naughty tale to tell, plucked from the pages of history. Tarted up, true, but guaranteed to stimulate the senses." While these lines (from Doug Wright's adaptation of his own play) prepare us for an erotic encounter, the camera gradually reveals an executioner at the guillotine. The public brutality counterpoints the purple prose of the Marquis de Sade: the woman is about to lose her head literally rather than figuratively. Kaufman invites the viewer into active participation with the film, foreshadowing both the sensuality and self-consciousness of subsequent scenes. And the opening of *The Queen* (2006) acknowledges that the function of a frame is to hold the picture and keep it in place. In a long take, Queen Elizabeth (played by Helen Mirren) poses for an official painting—an appropriate introduction to a character whose public image is imperious and immovable—before turning to the camera. As in his earlier film *Dangerous Liaisons* (1988), director Stephen Frears excels in female portraiture.

This approach to cinematic study is exploratory rather than exhaustive, a complement to approaches organized by theory, chronology, nationality, or genre. It originated in a course I introduced at Yale University and developed at Columbia; "Film Narrative" explores how movies from different countries tell a story in a uniquely cinematic manner. I organized the syllabus according to topics such as the Camera as Narrator, Meaningful Montage, Expressive Sound, Voice-Over Narration, and Black and White Versus Color, selecting films that illustrate the expressive power of cinematic elements. The one constant— despite differences of country, period, genre, directorial style, and story—was that the opening sequence provided the class with a fertile starting point for discussion. Instead of simplistic articulations of personal taste, the students had to begin with close analysis of the film, allowing the movie to lead them. The result (usually including a second screening of the first few minutes) was an elaboration of how cinematic language was utilized to tell the story.

Not all masterpieces boast an opening sequence that makes us sit up and take notice. Stanley Kubrick's *Paths of Glory* (1957), for example, has a straightforward introduction that is typical of classic Hollywood cinema: it sets up perfectly the movie's theme of military rigidity. Moreover, a few stunning sequences open films that do not live up to expectation. For instance, *The Naked Kiss* (1964) packs a wallop in its first two minutes as a scantily clad woman (Constance Towers) lunges at the camera, attacking a man. Even when he yanks off her wig and reveals her baldness, she keeps swinging. After knocking him to the ground, she takes exactly seventy-five dollars from his wallet and stuffs the cash into her black bra. However, Samuel Fuller's film later veers from vibrant rawness to implausible melodrama. And many classic movies need little explication to bring the viewer in. However, I am drawn to those films that benefit from close analysis. Whether it's the screenwriter or the director who is primarily responsible, the first scenes prepare us for a sophisticated appreciation of the motion picture that follows.

While this book covers only fictional films, a few superlative documentaries exhibit the same creative shaping, as exemplified by Joshua Oppenheimer's *The Look of Silence* (2015). This probing and moving companion piece to his *Act of Killing* (2012) returns to the continuing oppression and dishonesty of contemporary Indonesia vis-à-vis the murder of its own citizens in the late 1960s. The opening crystallizes a literal and figurative concern with perception: glasses with colored corrective lenses make us aware of the act of seeing.

Adi, who turns out to be both an optometrist and a quiet investigative figure, watches an older man singing on a TV monitor. Throughout the film, Adi asks discomforting questions to locals about the murders committed by death squads working for the military. They tell him he asks too many questions, preferring to live in metaphorical blindness, while he tries to clarify sight. As the son of a now-dead perpetrator later puts it, "Forget

FIGURE 1.1 From *The Look of Silence*

the past, and let's be happy like the military dictatorship taught us." But the footage of the past is too haunting, especially for Adi. And we cannot forget how the man in the TV tape of the opening laughs about choking someone, boasting—like the proud villains of Oppenheimer's previous documentary—of his violence.

The focus on beginning sequences leads to the inevitable question, when does the opening end? Whereas David Mamet proposed that an audience will give a film ten minutes, the precise amount of establishing time varies in each movie. Some start with a stylized prologue that is not really part of the action but sets a tone or introduces a theme, as in *Apocalypse Now* or *Raging Bull*. Both films truly have *overtures*, in that the music figures prominently, whether Italian opera or a song by The Doors. And many overtures are in fact credit sequences added by title designers. A fine mainstream example is *Dirty Dancing* (1987), whose writer and coproducer Eleanor Bergstein begins the DVD commentary by talking about the slow motion opening of different couples dancing sensually to the song "Be My Baby": "The film did not work until we came up with it. Richard Greenberg did the titles."[3] (Bergstein also added the voice-over of her teenaged protagonist "Baby," recalling, "That was the summer of 1963," setting the action prior to the assassination of John F. Kennedy and the Vietnam War.) Whereas her original vision incorporated only the "clean teen" music associated with "Baby" in the first scenes, "the credits let you know the dirty dancing is somewhere in the future," she explained.

In this context, graphic designer Saul Bass is a towering figure, having created Hitchcock's title sequences (and posters) of bold mobile grids for *Psycho* and hypnotic swirls for *Vertigo*. Jan-Christopher Horak's book *Saul Bass: Anatomy of Film Design* provides a comprehensive overview of the artist who gave a distinctive look to the opening of films including Otto Preminger's *The Man with the Golden Arm* (1955), *Anatomy of a Murder* (1959), and *Walk on the Wild Side* (1962), as well as Billy Wilder's *The Seven Year Itch* (1955).[4] His opening sequence for *Storm Center* (1956), in which Bette Davis plays a librarian who is labeled a communist after refusing to withdraw a controversial book from the shelves, is gripping: it shows the text of an open book over which a boy's eyes are superimposed. The extreme close-up of his glance moving laterally (and sometimes looking directly at the camera) is then menaced by flames at the bottom right of the screen. They slowly burn the pages until the frame is engulfed. This opening suggests not only the Nazis's book burning but the incendiary anticommunist hysteria of the 1950s. For *Seconds* (1966), directed by John Frankenheimer, Bass used evocative fragments of a distorted face to introduce the story of a man who fakes his death and undergoes plastic surgery toward a new identity. His masterful blending of haunting images with the kind of commercial exigencies found in advertising influenced such popular Hollywood franchises as the *Pink Panther* and James Bond movies, as well as Spielberg's *Catch Me If You Can* (2002) and the AMC television series *Mad Men*. His legacy is also visible in the strikingly crafted outer frames of contemporary titles designers.

Susana Sevilla Aho composed a probing video essay entitled "Things Are Not What They Seem" when she was a digital design student in 2013, tracing the evolution in motion graphic design from analog to digital ("remixed *visuality*"). With abundant clips, she explores the credit sequences from films by Hitchcock as well as David Fincher (often created by Kyle Cooper). Sevilla Aho compares Bass's superimposed graphics that introduce *North by Northwest* (1959)—a pioneering use of typography, with titles that are part of the landscape—to the oneiric credit sequence of *Se7en* (1995), whose fragments of a killer's notebook suggest the influence of experimental filmmaking.[5] Bass's work demonstrates how strong graphic design places the viewer in a self-consciously hybrid visual domain: when reality is abstracted before coming into focus, the fragments prepare spectators for an unfolding mystery.

Many of Pedro Almodóvar's movies begin with dazzling scenes that self-consciously reflect the Spanish director's delight in artifice. His international breakthrough was *What Have I Done to Deserve This?* (1984), a farce that cheekily undercuts conventions, shunning Spanish history as well as political correctness. Its colorful credit sequence is like an eyewink to the viewer, smacking of postmodern pastiche. Similarly, the titles of his immensely successful *Women on the Verge of a Nervous Breakdown* (1988) appear amid fragmentary images of red fingernails, lipstick, roses, and female figures from lingerie catalogues, accompanied by songstress Lola Beltrán's rendition of the ballad "*Soy infeliz*" (I am unhappy). *Talk to Her* (2002) reveals a greater

depth of both emotion and formal layering. Almodóvar's doubling and intersecting of two men's stories is bookended by
performances of the Pina Bausch Dance Company. The title
"HABLE CON ELLA" is printed on a curtain that rises to
reveal a stage: like sleepwalkers, two female dancers slowly, si-
lently, and despairingly knock against the wall as a man runs to
take chairs out of their way. In this staging of Bausch's *Café
Müller*, the women's closed eyes anticipate the film's recurring
image of a coma. Two men in the audience, seated together by
chance, observe this metaphor for mute imprisonment: Benigno
(Javier Cámara) turns out to be a nurse who is recounting the *Café
Müller* dance to a beautiful young woman in a coma; Marco (Darío
Grandinetti) is a writer enamored of a female bullfighter who
was gored by a bull. The act of storytelling links all the characters, whether verbally, visually (through dance, bullfighting,
and silent film), or musically (through an intimate performance
at a party of "Cucurrucucu Paloma" by Brazilian singer Caetano
Veloso). And the haunting score by Alberto Iglesias connects
Almodóvar's myriad time frames and emotional registers.

The role of music in creating a film's tone is equally crucial
to *Knife in the Water* (1962), the first feature directed by Roman
Polanski. Given that the Communist regime dismissed jazz as
a form of Western imperialism in his native Poland, the percussive and syncopated score by Krzysztof Komeda constitutes a
sensually defiant opening. (Censors initially shelved the film,
partly for its nihilism.) Offering no identifiable hero or even
forward progression, this portrait of three individuals—a bourgeois couple and a hitchhiker—on a boat is permeated with
frustration and futility, similar to that of Polanski's later films
such as *Rosemary's Baby*, *Chinatown*, and *The Pianist*. The first
shot is slightly above the windshield of a Mercedes moving on a
Polish road. Because this internal frame is both a window and a

mirror—reflecting the trees and therefore blocking our view of the man and woman inside the vehicle—we are made aware of our thwarted voyeurism. And since we cannot hear the dialogue as their lips move, the tension between the couple informs our own entrance into the film. Instead, the saxophone of Komeda's score invokes film noir (consistent with the black-and-white cinematography) and later adds a syncopation that expresses the film's offbeat relationships. The jazz score renders *Knife in the Water* a departure from traditional Polish cinema, closer to the experimentation of the French New Wave.

Polanski's compatriot Krzysztof Zanussi—a superlative director whose work explores political as well as moral compromise in a corrupt society—provides numerous examples of heightened credit sequences that create an edgy atmosphere. *Camouflage* (1976) is one of the best, opening with paintings of mammals and birds that adopt protective coloring. The tone of both the reptilian images and of Wojciech Kilar's score is simultaneously playful and ominous in introducing a linguistics conference being held by a provincial university at a summer retreat. The drawing of a snake is appropriate to the wily character of Jakub (Zbigniew Zapasiewicz), first seen setting traps and photographing birds. When he later dangles a real snake, Jakub seems to incarnate the figure of the devil. The object of his machinations is younger teacher Jarek (Piotr Garlicki), who is still idealistic about the system and his ability to navigate it. Jakub tempts him with the power that comes from cynical lucidity. The credit sequence prepares for the recurrence of animals throughout the film, suggesting a Darwinian vision rooted in the physical universe beyond the immediate frame of politics. The fact that *Camouflage* was not exported for almost two years means that censors understood Zanussi's use of metaphor and his own "protective coloring": if the animals of the opening represent politicians who mask their exterior, the turtle that accompanies Zanussi's title card as director illustrates the strongest protective surface.

To appreciate the primal role of a film's score, try watching the opening sequence with the soundtrack muted. In the case of Robert Altman's *McCabe and Mrs. Miller* (1971), to not hear Leonard Cohen's "The Stranger Song"—as Warren Beatty's character rides slowly into a wintry landscape on horseback—is to lose the movie's poetically poignant tone. Cohen's lyrics of melancholy and stream of minor-key guitar melodies merge with the fluidity of Vilmos Zsigmond's sweeping camera (in widescreen Panavision); Altman thus prepares the viewer for a stylized and personal tweak of the western genre. Similarly, Sergio Leone's spaghetti westerns are unimaginable without Ennio Morricone's sinuous music, which sets the stage for their breathless action as well as playful self-consciousness. For example, his theme for *The Good, The Bad and the Ugly* whisks together whistling, twanging guitar, and a man's "wa wa wa" sounds—filtering the epic quality of an American genre through Italian irony. In a different register, his score for *The Mission* (1986) is an exquisite aural expression of the counterpoints and resolutions between Jesuit priests and Guarani Indians in the mid eighteenth century.

The films of Federico Fellini derive much of their emotional impact from the music of Nino Rota. In *Amarcord* (1974), for example, his whimsical score functions as a literal overture accompanying the credit sequence, introducing the director's nostalgic and fantastical invocation of his childhood in the seaside town of Rimini. And the exuberant visual storytelling of Emir Kusturica is inseparable from the brassy, percussive rhythms of Goran Bregović: they vigorously set the tone in the opening sequences of Kusturica's memorable *Time of the Gypsies* (1988),

Arizona Dream (1993), and *Underground* (1995). Finally, one of the most justly celebrated examples is the title sequence designed by Balsmeyer & Everett for Spike Lee's *Do the Right Thing* (1989): on a hot Brooklyn street at night, Public Enemy's "Fight the Power" provides the kinetic pulse of Rosie Perez's defiant dance moves and introduces the film's incendiary quality.

‰ ‰ ‰

Given the eclectic taste on display in the following pages, it might be useful for the reader to know my criteria, even for films that are not part of this book—whose focus is on motion pictures made after 1959 and does not include such masterpieces as *Citizen Kane, Rules of the Game*, and *On the Waterfront*. I search for the internal coherence of the cinematic text (whether the movie succeeds on its own terms, as established by the opening) and for the film's resonance beyond the frame, which can be political, psychoanalytical, or cultural. When I was on the jury of the Berlin International Film Festival, our disparate group of artists and critics needed shared criteria for judging excellence. With the support of jury president Ben Kingsley, I proposed the following standards, which we adopted:

1. A meaningful or entertaining story, worth the proverbial price of admission
2. A cinematic language appropriate for the tale being told and, in the best of cases, a stretching of form that widens cinematic storytelling
3. A resonance that continues after the film is over—a philosophical or spiritual illumination of behavior that (forgive the potential corniness) makes us better human beings

Most mainstream films fulfill the first category; many art films expand on the second (a perfect example being *Hiroshima, mon amour*, whose fragmentary, elliptical editing style influenced countless motion pictures); and a precious few manage to stimulate us via the third as well. These include the films of Krzysztof Kieślowski (especially *The Decalogue* and *Three Colors*), Andrzej Wajda's *Ashes and Diamonds*, John Cassavetes's *A Woman Under the Influence*, and Philip Kaufman's *The Right Stuff*. Of course there are countless masterpieces from other geographical areas—notably China, India, Japan, and Scandinavia—that merit inclusion in a book of this kind, but I selected the countries and languages with which I have the greatest familiarity.

It might also be useful for readers to know what my critical tools are. Since my background is in literature, adaptation provides a point of departure. However, comparison to a novel can also cause derailment. When reading a book, each of us assumes the role of filmmaker. As words turn into images in our minds, we become not only the characters but also the camera eye. Perhaps that's why we rarely find a filmed version of a novel as satisfying as the book: the mental movie we make is necessarily more personal than the highly selective and condensed version of the director. Moreover, the very elements that make a novel shine—rich prose, tone, rhythm, and subjectivity—are the hardest to transpose to the cinematic medium.

In 1999 I attended a screening of the almost-final version of *The Talented Mr. Ripley*, introduced by writer-director Anthony Minghella. Since he also adapted *The English Patient* for the screen, Minghella had a solid basis for proclaiming, "The nature of adaptation is that it betrays as much about the adapter as about the source material."[6] Those seeking fidelity to beloved novels in the film versions are bound to be disappointed. Film adaptations betray a great deal about gifted filmmakers—namely their

concerns, from stylistic to thematic and moral. If we use literature and literary criticism as a model—for questions of narrative
structure, character development, imagery, rhythm, and authorial
point of view or intrusion—we can then develop a vocabulary
appropriate to film criticism.

There has always been a symbiotic relationship between books
and movies, and many of the greatest literary works are indeed
"cinematic." Those who appreciate the parallel tales of Paul
Thomas Anderson's *Magnolia* should be aware not only of the
pioneering work of Jean Renoir and Robert Altman with collective protagonists but also of D. W. Griffith; he, in turn, was
influenced by the parallel montage in the literature of Charles
Dickens and Gustave Flaubert. On the one hand, the novelist
E. L. Doctorow wrote, "Film de-literates thought; it relies primarily on an association of visual impressions or understand-
ings. Moviegoing is an act of inference. You receive what you
see as a broad band of sensual effects that evoke your intuitive
nonverbal intelligence. You understand what you see without
having to think it through with words."[7] On the other hand,
criticism is a function of returning these perceptual processes
to conceptual or articulable ones. And, ultimately, don't all narrative films adapt a verbal tale? Isn't there always a story set in
words—an idea, a treatment, a script—before the images over-
take linguistic constructs?

2

The Opening Translated from Literature

The Conformist, The Tin Drum, The Unbearable Lightness of Being, All the President's Men, Cabaret

---

In studying the opening of masterful adaptations like *The Conformist*, *The Tin Drum*, and *The Unbearable Lightness of Being*, we begin to explore the complex relationship between motion picture and viewer. Rather than being superficial or didactic, this relationship invites us to question how we see, especially when the director uses voyeurism self-consciously. And if the film is set in the past, it often leads us to see memory—or to visualize history—in a fresh way.

The students in my Senior Seminar in Film Studies at Columbia University read Milan Kundera's *The Unbearable Lightness of Being* after the first viewing of the movie made by Philip Kaufman in 1987; this permits us to better comprehend how the author and the director exploit the full resources of their respective art forms. Our vocabulary becomes descriptive rather than judgmental; instead of saying, "I liked the book better," we discuss how the film compresses the novel's narrative, shifts the point of view, and expands the frame. We accept that filmmakers treat a novel as raw material for a cinematic *translation*—a process of elucidation from one language (verbal) to another (audiovisual).

The technique of the flashback renders film the most supple medium to suggest causality from past to present—that our previous behavior and experiences determine our destiny (in a Freudian sense). The flashback structure implies fate: already "printed," events cannot but transpire as they do.

I begin with an Italian filmmaker, taking my lead from Millicent Marcus, who writes in *Filmmaking by the Book*: "Since postwar Italian film history is largely auteurist (in reaction to Fascist cinema, which presented itself as an authorless product of a system), I believe that a study of adaptation must concentrate on the filmmakers themselves."[1] She is particularly incisive when speaking of "umbilical scenes" through which "filmmakers teach us how to read their cinematic rewriting of literary sources." One of the supreme examples of a film shaped by flashbacks is *The Conformist* (1970), whose director, Bernardo Bertolucci, tells the story through uniquely cinematic means. Instead of falling back on the literary crutch of voice-over narration, he exploits expressive camera angles and movements, as well as color, visual texture, music, and contrapuntal editing. The author of the source novel is Alberto Moravia, whose work has been adapted by other major directors as well: Vittorio De Sica filmed his *Two Women*, and Jean-Luc Godard turned his *Ghost at Noon* into *Contempt*. If Moravia's novel unfolds chronologically via third-person narration, the film moves back and forth in time through the subjectivity of its protagonist. In December 1995 Bertolucci spoke at Lincoln Center's Walter Reade Theater during a retrospective of his work. About adapting *The Conformist*, he said, "I was flying over Moravia's pages as if they were a landscape, words like architecture."[2] Bertolucci's flash-back structure transforms the book into the first-person tale of Marcello (Jean-Louis Trintignant), who joins the secret Fascist police in Italy, partly to atone for what he thinks was a homo-sexual flirtation and murder in his youth. Marcello is assigned to kill his former professor Quadri—a Leftist in exile in Paris—while on his honeymoon there. But when he finds his old teacher, he is deeply attracted to Quadri's wife, Anna (Domi-nique Sanda), who seems drawn to both Marcello and his bride, Giulia.

The day of the assassination is the point of departure for a film about memory and desire. The opening sequence prepares the viewer for a vigorous engagement with the entire movie. During the credits, intermittent light makes us aware that we can't see everything. We discern a man sitting on a bed, but at moments the screen is black. The light—an evocative red—turns out to be a reflection from a neon movie marquee across the street: the title is *La Vie est à nous* (Life belongs to us), Jean Renoir's film of 1936. For those familiar with this celebration of the French Communist Party, the action of *The Conformist* unfolds in Paris before World War II and under the sign of self-conscious homage. We hear the lyrical melody of Georges Delerue's score as the man on the bed, fully dressed, becomes more visible. This will turn out to be Marcello, first glimpsed with his arm over his eyes. Bertolucci thus introduces the theme of sight, which will be developed throughout the film.

When Marcello gets up, the camera moves back a bit to reveal a hotel room as well as another person in the bed, naked and face down. Marcello approaches a bag in the left foreground and re-moves a gun: in front of a mirror, the close-up of his hand hold-ing the weapon separates it from the rest of his body—just as subsequent scenes will display his discomfort with a revolver. Is the other body we glimpsed alive or dead? A sleepy moan suggests the former. Male or female? Sexual ambiguity—one of the film's prominent themes—is thus introduced. Marcello removes his hat from a female posterior and covers the woman with a sheet. We subsequently learn that this is his bride, Giulia. The first scene suggests she is merely a physical prop for him and that Marcello is not comfortable with nudity; this impression is confirmed in a flashback where he visits his mother and covers her undressed body with a sheet. Throughout this opening sequence, Bertolucci acknowledges how he will reveal information only gradually, not allowing us to take anything for granted. We cannot ignore the indispensable contribution in this regard of cinematographer Vittorio Storaro, who collaborated with Bertolucci on subsequent films like *The Last Emperor* as well as with Francis Ford Coppola on *Apocalypse Now*, Warren Beatty on *Reds*, and Carlos Saura on a series of vibrant films about dance.

Accompanied by tense strings on the soundtrack, Marcello goes out to the dawn light and waits for a car. Again Bertolucci withholds information, forcing us to watch more attentively: we do not see who is speaking next to him, and we realize only afterward that Marcello is seated beside the chauffeur Manganiello, a tough, cigar-smoking, Italian-speaking Fascist. As they speed through the wintry landscape on this October day in 1938, flashbacks permit entry into Marcello's mind via a stream-of-consciousness narration. The first is to a recording studio, where he is superimposed on glass: we are seeing a reflection—a theme that will be developed explicitly and implicitly.

The most significant flashback takes us further back in time, to Marcello's childhood. He gets out of the car, takes a few steps ahead of it, and then holds up his arm to stop the car again. Suddenly we see a boy repeating the gesture in another time and place. The child Marcello gets into a lavish vehicle after being surrounded and perhaps attacked by other children. We cut to his confession to a priest—"I was thirteen," says the adult—before returning to his seduction by the handsome young chauffeur Lino in his room. The boy takes Lino's gun and finally shoots the chauffeur before fleeing through a window that magically opens. It is unclear whether he has killed Lino, but back in the confessional, Marcello says that Quadri's assassination will be the price he pays to society: he will kill "tomorrow" because "blood washes away blood."

Flashbacks within flashbacks render *The Conformist* a cinematic poem with internal rhymes. We keep moving from present to past because Bertolucci sees them as inseparable. Marcello is intent on becoming a conformist and Fascist in the present out of fear of what he might have done as a youth in the past. Sexual deviance and the possibility of being a killer exist both then and now. Marcello understands the connection between time periods only at the very end of the film, after the parade celebrating the downfall of Mussolini: upon hearing the voice of Lino, he realizes that he did not murder the homosexual chauffeur. He therefore sits down near a gay man in the Colosseum area. Marcello turns his head to the light from this prostitute's little bonfire—the flickering flame recalling the red reflection of the film's opening sequence—with a look that suggests both passion and illumination.

The Conformist is therefore, on a secondary level, a film about seeing. Its concentration on voyeurism leads to larger themes of blindness versus lucidity, shadows versus reality, and fascism versus individual morality. The theme of sight, introduced by the intermittent light of the very first shot, is developed through a few key scenes. In the first flashback, to the radio station, Marcello is with his friend Italo—a Fascist who happens to be blind. For Bertolucci, fascism equals blindness and Marcello

FIGURE 2.1 Marcello (Jean-Louis Trintignant) behind the windshield in *The Conformist*. All images in this book are digital frame enlargements taken directly from the BluRay or DVD versions of the films.

sees only reflections rather than "reality." When he later visits Quadri in Paris, they reenact Plato's myth of the cave, the famous parable about prisoners who are limited to perceiving reflections. The scene ends with the professor opening a window shade, letting in the light and erasing the shadows. The antifascist is thus the agent of illumination.

This is supported when Marcello subsequently recounts to Manganiello the dream he just had: with a windshield wiper in the hazy foreground, Marcello is framed behind the car's window. Through a shift of focus, his face fades as the wiper suddenly becomes sharply visible. This self-conscious visual manipulation suggests that perception is one of the film's key concerns: if a windshield wiper is that which clears vision, in this scene it becomes a metaphor for *The Conformist* as a whole. In Bertolucci's words, "Shooting the Plato scene, I had the feeling that the *cave* was talking about the invention of the cinema. Plato, not Lumière, is the inventor of the cinema. That exciting morning in 1970, we were still in the 1960s, with the idea that a movie not only had to tell a story, but investigate and analyze cinema—with the revolution made by the New Wave, especially Godard." The lighting throughout the film is self-consciously dramatic and often intermittent. For example, Marcello hits a swinging overhead lamp that casts momentary light in the back of a Chinese restaurant, expressing his wavering resolve about killing Quadri. Bertolucci proposes visually that we can see only what is illuminated for us. This is true not just for movie viewers but for citizens of any state: dictatorships don't reveal everything to the people. In interviews, he even admitted that he might be a fascist filmmaker because he manipulates everything we see. Is there not a form of fascism in the tyranny of our own expectations? But there is also great freedom in watching *The Conformist*: we are invited into active participation because we have to stay on our cinematic toes. Many shots are ambiguous, their meaning becoming apparent only in retrospect. Bertolucci adds to Moravia's story scenes of witnessing or peeping, choices that serve to make us aware of our own voyeurism; as a character in Bertolucci's *Before the Revolution* puts it, "Style is a moral fact."

It was after shooting *The Conformist* that Bertolucci decided to replace chronology with flashbacks. "I said to [Franco] Arcalli, my editor, 'Why don't we change the linear structure and make a long flashback?' Before, I called them 'the castrating scissors of the editors,' and I shot long takes that were impossible to intercut, like in *Partner*. But I shot the trip of Marcello and Manganiello in a way that could have become intercut." Bertolucci uses breathtaking cinematography, sensuous music, and deft montage, turning the verbal narration into an exploration of sexuality, politics, and cinematic style. We enter the tense rushes of Marcello's mind through flashbacks—moving from past to present and from fascism to freedom.

Bertolucci acknowledged his debt to the French New Wave, which ushered a new visual complexity into the early 1960s, augmented by the New German Cinema in the 1970s. By the end of that decade, it was possible for Volker Schlöndorff—a German-born, French-trained filmmaker—to use all the tools of the cinematic arsenal in bringing *The Tin Drum* to the screen. The Academy Award winner for Best Foreign-Language Film of 1979 is an epic, blending cinematic artistry, psychological insight, political vision, and a symbolic richness that defies any single interpretation.[3] The screenplay by Jean-Claude Carrière, Franz Seitz, and Schlöndorff is a remarkable reworking of Günter Grass's first book. It tells the story of Oskar Matzerath, who decides at the age of three to stop growing. He thus becomes a privileged witness to the rise of Nazism, which the film presents in terms of infantilism. It begins with a riveting sequence that has nothing to do with the novel's opening scene of a man observed behind a door's peephole.

In a vast field, a peasant woman allows a fugitive to hide under her huge skirts, even concealing from policemen his sexual penetration of her. She keeps eating potatoes, hot from the coals, while they pierce carts of potatoes with their bayonets. Once they leave, he emerges sheepishly from her clothing, zipping up his pants: she seems to have enjoyed the surprise and, in accelerated motion, they continue together through the field. The scene is audacious—not only in terms of the apparent rape, but also the presentation—fulfilling Carrière's assessment, "Bruegel meets Chaplin."[4] The cinematography of Igor Luther has a fairy-tale quality, slightly speeded up like celluloid in the silent era. Schlöndorff likened the effect to "a picture book for children" when he visited my film class at Columbia in 1987, adding, "Oskar wouldn't know how things looked before his birth, so we decided to use a camera of the time. But the lens for these cameras wasn't made for color stock. Because it wasn't color-corrected, we used a colorization filter." The haunting music of Maurice Jarre fulfills Schlöndorff's desire "to hear the earth-mother principle in the score," including a Jew's harp.[5] And the chilling voice-over narration of Oskar combines a child's timbre with an adult's comprehension. On a secondary level, it also reminds us of the film's literary origins.

Oskar conjures up a time before his birth, his omniscient voice occasionally suggesting a demonic presence. The opening image turns out to depict his own grandmother being impregnated by his grandfather. Schlöndorff thus introduces the themes of fecundity and adaptability that will recur throughout the film. In fact, the man crawling into the multiple skirts offers a reverse image of birth. By inventing the peasant woman, and ending *The Tin Drum* with the same figure, the film assumes a cyclical form that is quite different from the novel's linear structure. Schlöndorff thus foregrounds female continuity within nature, unlike Grass's focus on a solitary male. The film revels in elemental imagery, juxtaposing within one frame the nourishing earth, billowing smoke (fire and air), and finally water in the form of sudden rain.

Picking up on the novel's first image, the director uses an iris shot throughout the opening sequence—a black circle closing to end a scene, or an iris into the action to open the next scene—creating a peephole effect that grows comic. Oskar hypothesizes that his grandfather escaped and became a millionaire in Chicago—we therefore see the grandfather, Joseph, as a rich American—while his grandmother ages in Danzig, selling geese in the market. The final iris into a shot of the old woman shows that she now has a heated brick under her skirts—rather than a lusty man—to keep her warm. Thus, the opening sequence moves not only from a long shot of the landscape to close-ups of our characters but also from the smoke of the field to the contained fire of Joseph's cigar, to the muted heat of the brick.

The film's fresco then grows vast, bursting with juxtapositions of political and psychological acuity. Oskar narrates that he was born in 1924 Danzig, "between faith and disillusion," a time when a credulous people believed in Santa Claus—not realizing "that Santa Claus was really the gasman." Oskar (David Bennent, who was twelve when the film was shot) is the narrator of his own tale—a point of view dazzlingly reinforced by the use of subjective camera at his birth: the lens emerges from darkness to unfocused lights and sounds, finally delineating his mother, Agnes, and his two fathers (Agnes's husband, Alfred, and his biological father, Jan). Schlöndorff alternates between subjective and objective camera: in an eerie touch, the baby is also played by David Bennent. That he can see into the future is suggested by the superimposition of three-year-old Oskar with his drum onto the infant.

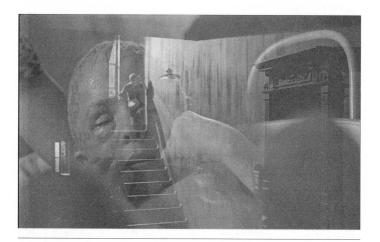

FIGURE 2.2 Oskar's birth in *The Tin Drum*

When he falls down the basement stairs at the age of three, the fall is expressed by a subjective camera that swirls around— just as it did when he was born—in slow-motion. We hear Oskar's piercing scream and also see him from the eerie perspective of a wide-angle camera underneath him. Oskar is, in a sense, giving birth to a new version of himself. In a Freudian context, he chooses to remain tiny after observing sexual contact between childish grown-ups; in 1945, at the age of twenty-one, he decides to grow again only after indirectly killing both his fathers. By this point, he is a father himself, and his son Kurt throws a rock at Oskar that leads him to fall. (The camera takes on a circular movement even before the little boy throws the stone, a visual echo of both Oskar's birth and his willful spiraling down the basement stairs.)

Throughout *The Tin Drum* eroticism is presented from a child's perspective as secretive: first, adults engage in concealed sex while eating potatoes or playing cards. Later, it is under the guise of "running errands" or crying, expressed through Schlöndorff's self-consciously voyeuristic camera angles. Agnes leaves Oskar in a toy store with Sigismund Markus (Charles Aznavour), but the child suspects that she is not going shopping and secretly follows her outside. Although he cannot see the hotel room where his mother and Jan (Daniel Olbrychski) fall into a heated embrace, the camera acts like an extension of his pulsating eyeball: we become privileged spectators, entering the room as if projections of Oskar's voyeuristic desire. His revenge is to climb to the top of a building, from which he emits a scream so loud that it shatters windows.

Once Oskar is of age (if not of size), he seduces the family servant Maria (Katharina Thalbach) with a fizz that is licked off one's palms. Indeed, the film is filled with images of people being fed (and often force-fed): after the opening of the peasant woman nibbling on a burning potato, a group of children give Oskar a nauseating "soup" that includes excrement, Alfred forces his wife to eat eels, and Oskar leads Alfred to swallow his Nazi pin when the Russians arrive. One of the film's most striking scenes is that of Agnes reeling from the sight of a severed horse's head on a beach: filled with eels, it is a stomach-churning image of birth as well as death. Moreover, it evokes another horrifying emblem of war, Picasso's *Guernica*.

The hallucinatory images of *The Tin Drum* lead us to question their meaning. For example, what of the title? Depending on one's perspective, it can refer to German militarism, a fiercely rebellious rejection of society, or an extension of the heartbeat that is a child's first sound in the womb. The film is designed to make the viewer think critically not only about images but also about history and human identity. On one level, Oskar is the symbol of resistance to fascism, denying responsibility in the debased world of adults. His primary activity is playing the tin drum, aggressively beating his own rhythm. At a Nazi rally his loud tempo subverts a military band until the scene grows comic: the rally becomes a dance as everyone suddenly waltzes to the Blue Danube! And he chooses to grow only after his country's last ties to Nazism have been severed.

The Tin Drum raises more questions than it can—or should— answer. They are not merely about the World War II era but also its aftermath. For example, Schlöndorff called Oskar a prophetic image of post-1968 youth: "His most important trait is his regressive attitude towards women. He wants to be everything with a woman, to be a lover, to be coddled like a baby, to dominate—only he cannot accept the grown-up male's responsibility towards women. This kind of attitude was prevalent in the thirties and is also widespread in the modern world. Oskar is obviously an ancestor of the post-'68 drop-out generation. The screaming of protests combined with the refusal to provide a realistic framework for change."[6] His diary entry of April 23, 1977—when he read *The Tin Drum* for the first time—recalls, "It could become a very German fresco, the history of the world seen from and lived on the bottom rung: enormous, spectacular paintings grouped together by the tiny Oskar." He succeeded magnificently in his aims, as Jack Kroll perceived in *Newsweek*: "A sizzling ferment of myth, epic, satire, political polemic, religious symbolism, transmuted autobiography and more."[7] The film ends as it began, with a peasant woman in a field. *The Tin Drum* thus presents a cyclical vision of life rather than a linear tale.

※ ※ ※

The screenwriter Jean-Claude Carrière would go on to collaborate on another masterful film, one rooted in the idea of eternal return as well as connections between the erotic body and the body politic. *The Unbearable Lightness of Being* was released in 1987, adapted from a screenplay that director Philip Kaufman cowrote with Carrière.[8] (This screenwriter was also Buñuel's accomplice, and his script collaborations include Daniel Vigne's *The Return of Martin Guerre*, Miloš Forman's *Valmont*, and Peter Brook's *Mahabarata*.) Its source is Milan Kundera's seemingly unadaptable novel of 1984, filled with philosophical asides about eroticism and mortality. Nevertheless—together with the cinematographer Sven Nykvist (best known for Ingmar Bergman's films)—they created an engaging visual tale as well as a complex meditation on voyeurism, politics, and morality. Its focus is Tomas (Daniel Day-Lewis), a philandering surgeon during the Prague Spring of 1968: he evolves from a playboy to a political hero when he refuses to sign a retraction demanded by Russian authorities. And his life is reshaped by Tereza (Juliette Binoche), who becomes his wife as well as a photographer. But he never renounces his mistress Sabina (Lena Olin), a bohemian artist who travels light, literally and figuratively. We follow our characters from the freedom of Alexander Dubček's regime, to exile in Switzerland, and back to the new heaviness of Soviet-dominated Czechoslovakia.

Carrière and Kaufman offered fascinating insights during a New York University symposium honoring the screenwriter on April 8, 2016. NYU's Center for French Civilization and Culture hosted a panel (at Cooper Union's Rose Auditorium) during which I was able to ask them about the process of adaptation. Carrière acknowledged that he wrote the first draft of the *Unbearable Lightness* screenplay in French (as he did for *The Tin Drum*). While working in a language other than the original novel permits a certain distance (valorizing plot over literary style), it also raises questions about how much translators can change original meaning. For example, Kaufman acknowledged that Kundera's title in French is *L'insoutenable légèreté de l'être*; the closest English word is not *unbearable* but *unsustainable*, invoking duration over time rather than heaviness. Similarly, Tomas's signature line in the film is "Take off your clothes"—a far more seductive invitation than the curt "Strip" command of the novel's English translation. Kaufman mentioned at the end of the panel that Kundera told him in Paris, "You must violate the book." The director's earlier playful remark, "A screenplay is a premeditation for a crime," invites speculation about the degree to which a film necessarily "violates" its source.[9]

Kaufman is repeatedly drawn to sophisticated material: after this film, he directed *Henry and June* (from the writings of Henry Miller and Anaïs Nin) as well *Quills*, about the Marquis de Sade. He acknowledged about *Unbearable Lightness*, "People would always say to us that the book seemed impossible to adapt. And they were right. The film is a variation on the book, a thread that comes from the book and leads back to the book. Maybe people who see the movie will refer to the book for references and reverberations."

A title card precedes the film's action: "In Prague, in 1968, there lived a young doctor named Tomas." Reminiscent of silent movies, the title introduces not only the protagonist but also his charged place and time in terms of sex and politics. In addition, its fairy-tale tone creates comic self-consciousness, heightened by the sense of a line translated into English from a foreign language. By having us "read" the screen, Kaufman thus begins not simply with an acknowledgment of a literary source but with a refusal of voice. This immediately separates his motion picture from Kundera's novel, which opens with the vocal speculation of the first-person narrator:

> The idea of eternal return is a mysterious one, and Nietzsche has often perplexed other philosophers with it: to think that everything recurs as we once experienced it, and that the recurrence itself recurs ad infinitum! What does this mad myth signify?
>
> Putting it negatively, the myth of eternal return states that a life which disappears once and for all, which does not return, is like a shadow, without weight, dead in advance, and whether it was horrible, beautiful, or sublime, its horror, sublimity, and beauty mean nothing."[10]

Instead, the film playfully celebrates the visual.

The opening sequence consists of five scenes, beginning with a spark: a beautiful nurse strikes a match to light a cigarette, virtually igniting the film. "Take off your clothes," Tomas says to her from under a towel. As she complies, the camera pulls back to reveal that they are visible to a patient lying on the other side of the window, as well as a doctor standing next to him. With our own voyeurism shared by secondary characters, Kaufman invites our gaze at the same time that he makes us aware of internal frames. The juxtaposition of eroticism and self-consciousness continues in the second scene, introduced by the title "But the woman who understood him best was Sabina." Tomas and this beautiful artist lie on her bed, his head covering her naked breast. Her bowler hat hides part of her face. As they move more fully into view, their lovemaking includes a vividly visual dimension: the oval mirror next to the bed not only permits them to look at themselves but also opens up another plane for the audience as well, reflecting itself into the heart of the frame. Kaufman thus invokes eternal return in a cinematic manner, the image repeating itself infinitely. It is noteworthy that Tomas and Sabina are laughing while making love, displaying an erotic jocularity rare in motion pictures.

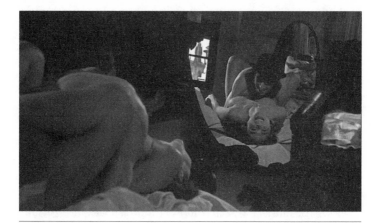

FIGURE 2.3 Tomas (Daniel Day-Lewis) and Sabina (Lena Olin) in *The Unbearable Lightness of Being*

The credits unfold in the third scene, as Tomas drives from Prague to a spa town. After a close-up of his eyes behind dark glasses, he removes them and we see his gaze. Kaufman thus continues the motif of interrupted sight: we move from Kundera's text (an abstraction) to visual obstruction—whether a towel, a hat, a head, or sunglasses—followed by revelation. Later, during a frankly erotic scene, Sabina straddles the mirror on the floor and asks Tomas, "What are you looking at?" He replies, "Your eyes." Kaufman does indeed replace the "I" of Kundera's text with the "eye" of cinematic storytelling—an appropriate substitution for a work that alludes more than once to Sophocles's *Oedipus Rex*. And it is eye contact that brings Tomas together with Tereza when he visits her spa town to perform an operation.

Kaufman's locale is redolent of steam baths, where an off-screen massage evokes sounds indistinguishable from sexual moans. At the center is a swimming pool, where Tomas observes six men around a floating chessboard—an image of male strategy that is suddenly disrupted by the graceful dive of a female body. Tomas's gaze follows her underwater glide through the pool, and then to the curtain behind which she dries herself with a towel. Watching the silhouette of her naked body, Tomas then follows her—through the mist-filled corridors of the spa—into the café where she is a waitress. There, her own eyes (in a subjective shot) find Tomas, who pretends to be reading. By the time they finally speak, the atmosphere is charged with the simmering sexual attraction between Tomas and Tereza. In a departure from the novel, their eyes suggest desire—or free will—rather than chance. Enhancing the novel, Kaufman anchors the metaphysical in the gloriously physical.

Using the music of Czech composer Leoš Janáček, he provides a structure that could be called musical: over its three-hour running time, the film moves from andante to adagio, from light—visually and thematically—to dark, and from quick cuts to longer takes. While Kundera's book has a musical form as well—a kind of theme plus variations—the experience of the two works is quite different. Kundera urged Kaufman to "eliminate" whenever possible, aware that an adaptation of his novel could not be faithful. The director therefore enjoyed a degree of freedom that permitted him to shift the focus of the book from a philosophical rumination to a love story. Moreover, like Bertolucci with *The Conformist*, Kaufman explores not just voyeurism but perception as well. He adds numerous mirrors, windows, and curtains to the screenplay, making us aware of what is hidden as well as what is revealed. How much are we allowed to see—by the filmmaker? by the state? (After all, the setting includes the Soviet invasion.) And by ourselves? Tereza, for example, tells of her nightmare that Tomas made her watch him with other women (an involuntary voyeurism). And in the context of "the unbearable lightness of being," the film also seems to ask whether to be seen is to be less light.

At the NYU symposium Kaufman articulated how he and Carrière arrived at the film's opening by likening it to "the garden hose in my backyard that curls around. We said, 'Let's find out what these repeated motifs are,'" leading to "a structure like an overture at the beginning." Indeed, a film's introduction is an often self-conscious framing device that prepares the viewer for multiple motifs as well as a heightened awareness of the cinematic storytelling. The literally striking way *All the President's Men* begins provides a fine illustration: director Alan J. Pakula enhances both the image and sound of typewriter keys, as words will indeed be weapons in his drama about Watergate. It was released in 1976, a mere two years after Nixon's resignation as US president, a direct result of the Watergate break-in of 1972.

FIGURE 2.4 From the opening scene of *All the President's Men*

The white screen is held blank and silent for an extra few seconds, creating an expectation. It is filled by words that register like gunshots, appropriate to the story of newspapermen. The soundtrack layers whiplashes and gunshots to heighten the intensity of typewriter keys striking paper. Similarly, when a teletypewriter prints headlines in the closing sequence, we hear in the background—from a television—cannon fire of a twenty-one-gun salute celebrating Nixon's second inauguration.

Archival footage then situates us in a very particular historical moment, when Nixon—at the peak of his popularity—was returning from a historic trip to China. The rest of the film will be characterized by an urgent realism—for example, in the multitrack sound design of the massive *Washington Post* newsroom. Pakula reconstructs the investigation conducted by the reporters Bob Woodward and Carl Bernstein—played by Robert Redford and Dustin Hoffman—that led to their book. Using William Goldman's screenplay adaptation, *All the President's Men* recounts a domestic political tale of the 1970s, utilizing a relatively classical style that links it to a Hollywood tradition boasting directors like Howard Hawks, Frank Capra, and William Wyler. If the causality of events engenders a straightforward narration, other films of the 1970s tended toward a greater stylization.

Victor Brombert proposes that all openings, specifically in the realist novel, serve to simultaneously create an illusion of realism and to undermine the notion of mimetic representation.[11] *Cabaret* (1972) offers a superb cinematic elaboration of this dual tendency. Directed by Bob Fosse, it was based on Christopher Isherwood's *Goodbye Berlin* (published in 1939), from which John Van Druten adapted a stage play, *I Am a Camera*, in 1951; it led to a 1955 film version, and then a stage musical entitled *Cabaret* in 1966. To add another temporal layer, it is set in the pre-Nazi past of 1931 Berlin. This musical drama is entertaining, engrossing, and ultimately chilling in its stylized tableaux of spreading swastikas. Fosse's Master of Ceremonies (Joel Grey) leads us into the world of the film.

The credits unfold over a dark background that gradually comes into focus (like the film's concerns), a distorted mirror that

FIGURE 2.5 The MC (Joey Grey) in *Cabaret*

reflects the cabaret clientele like a grotesque painting by George Grosz. Into the eerie-looking glass pops the painted face of our depraved guide. He welcomes not only the patrons of the Kit Kat Klub but also the film's viewers, especially when he sings "Willkommen." Appropriate to the opening, the ensuing musical numbers reflect, comment upon, and often parody the growing influence of the Nazis. The distorted reflection corresponds to the musical productions, which are consistently crosscut with the political reality outside.

"Life is a cabaret, old chum," sings Sally Bowles, but the cabaret is also life, translated into spectacular reflection. Like the club's patrons, we enter this musical world to forget about reality, only to find that it cannot be kept outside. The last image of the film will be the misshapen mirror of the first shot, now reflecting a profusion of swastika armbands on cabaret patrons. Like the other adaptations in this chapter, *Cabaret* builds on a gripping opening sequence that exploits a cinematic expressiveness born of literary articulation.

3

Narrative Within the Frame

Mise-en-Scène and the Long Take

Touch of Evil, The Player, Aguirre: The Wrath of God, The Piano, Bright Star, In Darkness

M y understanding of film history and language was shaped by the theorist André Bazin, whose essays celebrate the unity of time and space in motion pictures.[1] He opposed how montage fragments the world, especially in the Russian tradition of Sergei Eisenstein, and praised directors like Jean Renoir and Roberto Rossellini who utilized long takes. Because quick editing dominates moviemaking today—reflecting as well as feeding attention deficit disorder—I share with my students inspirational examples of uninterrupted long takes: these allow meaning to inhere and grow within the image, especially at the start of a film. *The Godfather* (1972) provides a fine example: Francis Ford Coppola begins with the words "I believe in America," spoken by an Italian-American immigrant in close-up. As the camera slowly pulls back, we see that he is asking a favor of Don Corleone (Marlon Brando), initially identified only through a slight wave of his hand. The long take then cuts to the godfather, Corleone, elegantly seated at his desk, and later to the shuttered room, gradually revealing a few of his men who have been listening to the conversation. Corleone turns the situation to his advantage: this man will be in his debt. The scene has established the quiet and extensive power not only of the title character but also of the filmmaker: the rhythm of both is unhurried and cumulatively dramatic. This renders *The Godfather* not simply a gangster film but an epic exploration of the American dream.

My Bazinian appreciation of long takes is not mutually exclusive with respect for montage. For an evocative classic Hollywood opening sequence, see *The Letter*, directed by William Wyler in 1940. A quick shot of the full moon provides a cosmic frame for the introduction of a murder. After a road sign establishes the location as the Rubber Company in Singapore, the camera tilts down a tree from which sap pours into a bucket, then pulls back into a wide shot of the plantation, tracking up and to the right, past workers sleeping. It continues to rise and circle as we hear the tinkling music of Max Steiner, which stops with the sudden sound of a gunshot. As Bette Davis's Leslie shoots a man multiple times—descending the steps to her house—we hear indistinct sounds of men who work there and barking dogs. The camera moves into a close-up of her implacable face before clouds cover the moon. Wyler effectively creates not only tension and mystery but also narrative complicity: the protagonist's lethal act has been heard by those who work on the plantation, but only we have seen her shoot. Will she get away with murder? From the moon to the fecund tree, nature is a witness.

The touchstone of uninterrupted long takes is *Touch of Evil*, even if Orson Welles's dark thriller was initially dismissed when Universal released it in 1958. Reviewers considered it confusing, and while Welles's pulpy B movie might still merit such an adjective, it is also now a cult classic. A star was needed to play the policeman Vargas, and Charlton Heston agreed (cast somewhat against type as a Mexican, given his other roles at that time—Moses and Ben Hur). The casting of Janet Leigh as his wife invites intriguing speculation about the degree to which *Touch of Evil* might have influenced Hitchcock in making *Psycho* with the same actress less than two years later. In both films an assault on Leigh takes place in a motel; moreover, the circular motif on the motel wall of Welles's film becomes part of the imagery of *Psycho*, culminating in the drain of Hitchcock's famous shower sequence.

Universal had editor Robert Wise cut Welles's version while the director was in South America making another film. Forty years later, Walter Murch oversaw the 1998 restoration of *Touch of Evil*, using Welles's original fifty-eight-page memo intended to bring the studio's cut in line with the director's intentions.[2] The opening shot consists of a 3 minute, 20 second unbroken take that establishes the camera as a mobile narrator. There is not only self-conscious virtuosity here but also the introduction of stylistic and thematic elements that will be developed throughout the film. The black-and-white lighting is narratively organic: cinematographer Russell Metty often creates shadows in front of the characters. Their moral ambiguity is expressed by the intermittent illumination—the play of dark and light—around them. The camera actively follows a hand, a car, and then two couples crossing paths as they approach the border between Mexico and California. As the camera moves from a close-up of hands setting a bomb, it creates tension and suggests the forces that tick away under the surface of relationships. The man who sets the bomb runs away, followed by his shadow on a wall (an expressionistic detail that recalls film noir), and the camera then rises after the bomb is placed. It moves away from the car

FIGURE 3.1 Vargas (Charlton Heston) and his wife (Janet Leigh) walking in front of a car in *Touch of Evil*

to reveal the Mexican border town, which gradually fills up with people: the frame expands to encompass pedestrians and even goats, establishing multiple axes of vision. The camera descends to follow Heston and Leigh, who pass the car. This intersection leads us to fear not only for the couple in the car (the targets of the ticking bomb) but also for the "innocent" pedestrians.

The soundtrack is equally potent: the bomb is set in silence, interrupted by a woman's off-screen laughter. The diegetic music emanating from the Mexican bars and streets is then juxtaposed with American rock music from the Cadillac. At the border, we hear overlapping conversations, like the woman in the car complaining of the ticking in her head while the officer asks about the Grande case. This is all in one take, maintaining tension and spatial unity. After the bomb explodes, the film shatters into fragments. If we assumed our protagonist would be either Heston or Leigh, Welles undercuts this assumption with the introduction of Hank Quinlan, played by the director himself as a grotesque, overweight, and possibly corrupt cop. Quinlan plants evidence in order to arrest a Mexican man—whose girl-friend is white—for the crime of the opening scene. With the explosion, the film's first cut is visually engendered by the kiss of Leigh and Heston, a blonde American woman and a Mexican male. The borders of this late 1950s film are not only geographical but ethnic, including Caucasian and Latino. The borders are also moral, legal, and always blurred. Ultimately, *Touch of Evil* explores a boundary between civilization and primitive instinct. Welles crosses visual and narrative borders as well, lacing a linear story with internal rhymes, like the intersecting couples of the opening shot. The last film Welles made in Hollywood, *Touch of Evil* is now recognized as a fusion of pulp art and continental sophistication, as well as one of the most formally rich American movies of the late 1950s. And it provides a connection to the French New Wave, given its showing at the 1958 Brussels World's Fair Film Festival. The jury included two young French film critics, François Truffaut and Jean-Luc Godard, who voted *Touch of Evil* best film.

Robert Altman pays homage to Welles's movie explicitly and implicitly in *The Player* (1992), where a security guard (Fred Ward) criticizes the "cut-cut-cut" of recent films and invokes the opening of *Touch of Evil*. The camera moves on a horizontal axis in an uninterrupted long take that is not only self-conscious but also inclusive. The fluidity of the camera constantly reframes, rendering the frame itself malleable rather than fixed. Altman's provisional frame contains a myriad of characters, thereby emphasizing a collective protagonist, or interdependence, much as he did in *Nashville*. The camera eye is autonomous and self-aware: it fulfills our desire to see in long shot as well as close-up, encompassing totality and detail. Since *The Player* is set in a film studio, this self-consciousness is appropriate. Working from Michael Tolkin's novel and script, Altman's film centers on a

FIGURE 3.2 Buck Henry pitching a film to Griffin (Tim Robbins) in *The Player*

Hollywood executive who receives death threats from a writer whose script he rejected. The shout of "Action" heard off-screen engenders the camera within as well as beyond the frame; it pulls back from the studio doors, rises, and then descends to the arriving car of Griffin (Tim Robbins), the executive to whom everyone will pitch movie ideas, including Buck Henry (who cowrote the screenplay of *The Graduate*) proposing "The Graduate, Part II" starring Julia Roberts as the daughter. A German poster of *The Blue Angel* can be glimpsed on Griffin's office wall, suggesting that he has taste. Jeremy Piven (who would play the Hollywood agent in HBO's *Entourage*) is the tour guide for a group of Japanese visitors. When the film was released, Julie Salamon wrote in the *Wall Street Journal*, "This brilliant satire, styled as a murder mystery, is the best insider's view of Hollywood since 'Sunset Boulevard.'"[3]

From Altman's horizontal axis of vision, we move to the vertical axis of *Aguirre, the Wrath of God*. A motion picture of lyrical as well as terrifying poetry, it was directed by Werner Herzog in

1972. He recreates a doomed expedition of 1560 into the Peruvian jungle by a conquistador who was searching for the lost city of El Dorado, city of gold. In 1979 the director said he had become increasingly obsessed by "a primordial innocence of vision."[4] Even if a few have questioned Herzog for risking lives in the pursuit of his visions, he was hailed as the leading filmmaker of the New German Cinema. His hallucinatory, quasi-anthropological movies have brought attention to remote cultures and marginalized individuals. Some are documentaries, such as *La Soufrière*—about a volcano that he personally explored, despite its imminent eruption—while others were fictional, like *The Enigma of Kaspar Hauser*. Herzog has been drawn to people on the verge of extinction, from aboriginal tribes in Australia, to the Miskito Indians of Nicaragua, and more recently to American inmates on death row. *Aguirre* is based on the actual diary of a monk named Gaspar de Carvajal. In the opening sequence, the

FIGURE 3.3 The mountain descent that opens *Aguirre, the Wrath of God*

images and music express a physical descent—and perhaps a metaphysical one—through a primeval natural landscape.

Herzog's slow pace allows each image to sink in during the elemental introduction: anchored by the mountain (earth), we see the sky above, the mist to the right invoking water, and finally fire after the crash of a cannon. The very shape of the mountain descent will be rhymed by a lightning bolt (which could be interpreted as the wrath of God). This locale in Peru is the most famous icon of Inca civilization. (The high priest and local virgins lived on its peak.) The physical effort of the actors making their way down the mountain fulfills what the film-maker Barbet Schroeder once said on a Telluride Film Festival panel: all movies are documentaries in the sense that they record real people doing real things.[5] Here, we see animals in addition to the indigenous people and the European men in heavy breastplates making the arduous descent. The scene anticipates Herzog's 1982 *Fitzcarraldo* (also starring Klaus Kinski), the epic tale of a nineteenth-century Irishman whose attempt to build an opera house in the Brazilian jungle led him to lug a boat up a mountain (which we see recreated on-screen in painstaking detail, without the benefit of CGI).

The descent of tiny beings down the mountain of *Aguirre* is accompanied by the hypnotic music of Florian Fricke, using the name Popol Vuh (from the Mayan creation myth). Herzog explained to Roger Ebert, "We used a strange instrument, which we called a 'choir-organ.' It has inside it three dozen different tapes running parallel to each other in loops. . . . All these tapes are running at the same time, and there is a keyboard on which you can play them like an organ so that [it will] sound just like a human choir but yet, at the same time, very artificial and really quite eerie." Moreover, throughout the film the score's use of fifths conveys the sense of something missing in the middle.

Herzog's passion for music is evident in the hypnotic soundtracks of his movies, which often rise and fall alongside a character's ascent or descent. Whether it is a mountain climber in *The Dark Glow of the Mountains* (1984), a ski jumper in *The Great Ecstasy of Woodcarver Steiner* (1974), Stroszek on a stalled ski lift, or Fitzcarraldo pulling a boat up the impossibly steep slopes, the scores of his films express a longing for flight or transcendence. (It is not surprising that Herzog went on to direct opera.)

The voice-over narration of the monk provides another narrative layer in *Aguirre*, bringing Herzog's tale back to oral traditions. This voice will turn out to be deceptive: the narrator is killed before the end of the film. *Aguirre* shares with other masterful films the tension between a linear, progressive journey and a spiraling downward. Indeed, *Apocalypse Now* seems inspired by some of Herzog's thematic and stylistic brio. The beginning of *Aguirre* can move from heaven to earth, but by the end of the film the camera only goes around in circles. The last shot is as striking as the opening: from the whirling camera we see the demented, lopsided Aguirre alone on his raft, in command only of corpses and hundreds of chattering little monkeys. It invokes the image of the whirlpool that dominates an earlier sequence. Listening to the film's German dialogue provides another layer of meaning. When Kinski's conquistador character says, "We need a leader," using the word "führer," the film becomes a postwar meditation on German guilt. He proclaims, "We'll produce history as others produce plays." If the characters in this primordial landscape search for gold, it is power that Aguirre really seeks. As Ebert wrote, "Of modern filmmakers, Werner Herzog is the most visionary and the most obsessed with great themes. . . . He wants to lift us up into realms of wonder. Only a handful of modern films share the audacity of his vision; I think of "*2001: A Space Odyssey*" and "*Apocalypse Now*."[6]

When Werner Herzog visited my class at Yale University in the 1980s, he proposed that anyone making a film should try to fulfill two goals—to establish a new grammar of images and to define our human situation. These aims inform countless motion pictures, especially those that invite the viewer to grapple with images at the outset. Memorable opening sequences are not merely dazzling eye-openers but narrative guides that respect and reward active curiosity. Jane Campion's work provides numerous examples, including the now classic Academy Award winner *The Piano* (1993) and the lesser-known *Bright Star* (2009). Economically as well as enigmatically, she introduces her female protagonists through visual and aural details—particles moving against a black frame—that need to be deciphered. In *The Piano* hazy vertical digits could be fingers or perhaps piano keys. As the female voice-over begins, a close-up of fingers covering a face—except for an open left eye—foregrounds the act of looking. The charged gaze will indeed recur throughout the film, often making voyeurism discomforting. As Campion crosscuts between the cryptic dark frame and the facial close-up (where a wedding band is noticeable), she creates a counterpoint between subjective and objective camera: in retrospect it becomes clear that the hazy verticals are from the point of view of the character simultaneously peeking through her fingers and hiding behind them. Her protagonist's narration supports this duality: "The voice you hear is not my speaking voice but my mind's voice. I have not spoken since I was six years old." Ada (Holly Hunter) sounds childlike, with a Scottish lilt, perhaps because this voice has not been heard since she was six. Like Oskar in *The Tin Drum*—who chose to halt his growth at the age of three—Ada refused to completely enter adulthood. And if the German boy's identity was inseparable from his drum, the piano is the voice of Campion's heroine, expressing her lyricism, control, and passion.

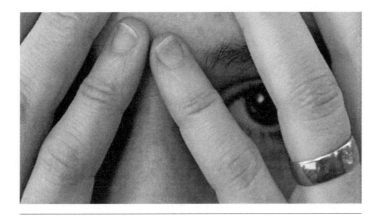

FIGURE 3.4 The gaze of Ada (Holly Hunter) in *The Piano*

We then see Ada seated under a tree, watching a little girl learning to mount a horse; her intermittent gaze might be that of a mother apprehensive for her child's safety. The external landscape leads to visual expansion: the camera rises to a high angle, following Ada as she walks among the leaves. (The stunning cinematography is by Stuart Dryburgh.) The next shot establishes horizontal mobility as well: her daughter, Flora (Anna Paquin), glides on roller skates through a corridor. Her skating engenders the fluid motion of the camera floating into Flora's room, where Ada puts the skates back under the child's bed. While the camera's point of view is no longer that of Ada, it is an extended subjectivity that depends neither on the lens being identified with her eye nor on a close-up of her face, as her consciousness is expressed by the mise-en-scène. Ada's voice-over reveals that she is embarking on a voyage for an arranged marriage. (The camera is revelatory as well: when she sits down at the piano, it circles around her to show that the actress is really playing the stirring music we hear, composed by Michael Nyman.)[7]

From Scotland we move to the rugged beach of New Zealand, where Ada and nine-year-old Flora are stranded with their heavy belongings. When her new husband, Stewart (Sam Neill), arrives, he says they cannot take the piano, which remains on the beach. As Columbia University student Christina Crisostomo wrote in an unpublished paper of May 2016:

> Although there is very little in her life that she can control—having been sold to a stranger and unable to stop the sale of her beloved instrument—when she is seated before her piano, she is the master of herself. It's why the scene of her husband ordering his men to leave the piano behind on the beach is devastating, as she is stripped of her true voice. The music that plays over this scene, as well as during several other high emotional points in Ada's story, is arguably her theme song. It's called "The Heart Asks Pleasure First" and it takes its name from an Emily Dickinson poem about choosing death over steadily increasing pain. This literary reference gains relevance when one considers the scene near the end, where Ada—grieving over the loss of her finger and thus, her true self (or what she perceived to be her true self)—nearly chooses to drown with her piano. The turbulent music embodies the passions simmering just beneath the surface of her character.[8]

Baines (Harvey Keitel), a tattooed neighbor who has adopted the Maori life, offers to bring her the piano—one black key for every lesson—if she allows him to do certain things while she plays it. First, Baines kisses the back of her neck. Then he sits under her lifted skirts. Later, the film's eroticism blossoms as he removes his clothes. But Campion does not permit pure titillation. At the very moment that our voyeurism is most keen, their nude bodies are depicted from the perspective of Flora and then through the pained eyes of her husband. As a result, in humiliation Stewart almost rapes her in the forest. But the violation shown in parallel montage is even greater for Ada—Maori men playing her piano.

Ada sends her daughter to Baines with a wooden note plucked out of the piano, on which she has written that he has her heart. But Flora gives it to Stewart. His rage leads him to chop off one of Ada's fingers—juxtaposed with the removal of a piano note (which returns us to the ambiguity of digits in the opening). This invokes a show that was staged for a Maori audience earlier in the film; it made them believe so completely in the illusion that they stormed the stage to stop a man behind the screen from bringing an ax down on a woman. We are perhaps no less impressionable, taken in by Campion's spectacle, hoping to stop the ax. Perhaps like Ada in the opening scene, we simultaneously cover one eye and peer out the other.

Bright Star dramatizes the intense love affair that developed between poet John Keats (Ben Whishaw) and neighbor Fanny Brawne (Abbie Cornish). Aged twenty-three, the shy, sickly poet seems a dubious match for the eighteen-year-old witty, gregarious seamstress/designer. But the heightened tactility associated with her from the opening shots—extreme close-ups of a needle stitching material as we hear voices singing in harmony—is later rhymed by the sharpness of his quill moving across paper. After the abstract shots of the needle piercing cloth, we see the woman seated to the left of a window that provides the only illumination in a dark room: Fanny wields her needle expertly. Although she seems to be alone, a shape on the right moves: her younger sister gets up from bed to watch her. Campion calls attention to the process of creation, whether the action is sewing

fabric, crafting verse, or making a movie. The film is richly tex-
tured, both visually (as in an early tableau of white sheets waving
in front of the house) and aurally (mostly Mozart). For example,
a male a cappella chorus performs at a party—each section
taking on the responsibility of an instrument—which provides a
sound bridge to a scene of Fanny's dancing lesson with a French
instructor.

Bright Star is not just the tale of the brief but inspirational
love of two engaging real-life individuals. As the second half of
the opening sequence implies, Keats's best friend—Mr. Brown
(Paul Schneider), a Scottish poet—is a crucial figure. When
Fanny and her family visit friends with whom Keats is staying,
the verbal sparks between Brown and Fanny suggest that they
are the real opposites who are attracting. "Ah, the very well
stitched little Miss Brawne, in all her detail," he needles, before
blowing smoke. She responds by dismissing his poems: "They
puff smoke, dissolve, leaving nothing but irritation." Later in the
film, she calls the color of his eyes "suitcase brown"; this leads
him to send her a valentine, over which Keats explodes in jeal-

FIGURE 3.5 Fanny Brawne (Abbie Cornish) in *Bright Star*

ousy. Although Brown claims it was a joke and always seems eager to banish Fanny from their writing enclave—"Desist or depart," he commands—the intensity of their repartee suggests otherwise. Ultimately, Brown is perhaps the most tragic character. Whereas Keats dies young but having known love and penned sublime poetry, Brown has lost not only his best friend and writing partner but also his freedom and future, settling for marriage to a maid he impregnated.

As in *The Piano*, Campion's focus is on a brave woman who is always accompanied by a young girl (Fanny's sister, Toots). And the director once again uses cinematic language expressively. For example, a shot of Fanny before an open window, the curtain lifted by the breeze, suggests her emotional ascent through love. When Keats must leave, she—with her younger brother and sister—catches butterflies and keeps them in her room. They externalize the fluttering within her, while foreshadowing the short life of these winged feelings. Campion gives visual form to Keats's achingly beautiful poetry: "Awake forever in a sweet unrest," he says at Fanny's breast, in a poem that will become "Bright Star." And he could be speaking inspirational lines for filmmakers like Campion when he says, "Poetry soothes and emboldens the soul to accept mystery."

Although Campion is among the very few female filmmakers who have achieved international prominence, Agnieszka Holland is another beacon of hope, especially for her drama *In Darkness* (2011). She is not just one of Poland's leading directors and screenwriters but also a truly international filmmaker: among her credits are the Oscar-nominated *Europa, Europa* and *Angry Harvest* (both primarily in German); the French-language *Olivier, Olivier*; *The Secret Garden* and *Washington Square* in English; and episodes of American cable TV series including *The Wire* and *Treme*. *In Darkness* is based on Robert Marshall's 1991 book *In the*

Sewers of Lvov, which expanded his 1988 documentary for the BBC, *Light in the Dark*—both of which inspired screenwriter David F. Shamoon. The film is magnificently photographed by Jolanta Dylewska—herself a documentary filmmaker, notably of *Chronicle of the Warsaw Ghetto Uprising According to Marek Edelman* (1993). While visually rich, *In Darkness* is far from sentimental. The focus of this true story is Leopold Socha (Robert Więckiewicz), a Polish sewer worker and petty thief who ends up becoming a reluctant savior of eight Jews in hiding.[9] It is set in 1943 Nazi-occupied L'vov, a Polish city that became Ukrainian thanks to the Hitler-Stalin pact. Unlike most Hollywood movies, the film has a linguistic authenticity, with characters speaking Polish, German, Yiddish, and Ukrainian.

As in Holland's *Angry Harvest* (1985), the protagonist is initially enticed by material gain but ultimately risks his life when he grows to care about the victims (who are hunted by both the Nazis and the Ukrainians) during the fourteen months they spend in the sewers after escaping the liquidation of the ghetto. Reminiscent of Holland's screenplay for Andrzej Wajda's underrated 1990 drama *Korczak*, this portrait of a savior explores relationships between Polish Christians and Jews, undermining simplistic stereotypes about the former being anti-Semites or the latter being meek. (While Holland's father was Jewish, she has often said that her appreciation of Jewish identity came from her Christian, philo-Semitic mother.) Some uneducated Christian characters don't realize Jesus was Jewish, but Socha's wife, Wanda (Kinga Preis), represents a basic level of decency, expressing pity for the Jews. Even though she and their daughter leave Socha because they fear his life-risking actions on behalf of the victims, she returns. Similarly, brave Jewish characters like Mundek (Benno Fürmann) lead Socha to acknowledge his misperception, "And I always thought Yids were cowards."

The first image—a toy train and figurines, suddenly illuminated by the flashlight of a thief—introduces numerous elements. The contrast of light and dark is striking, establishing partial illumination of a dark frame as the norm. Self-reflexivity is heightened, as we are made aware of watching a miniature representation (and later in the film, an officer records a street near the L'vov Ghetto). When the younger thief, Stefek (Krzysztof Skonieczny), looks at the train with childlike amazement, the theme of innocence coexists with robbery and the eventual hell of sewers. Finally, the thieves are surprised by the sudden appearance of a Polish girl and her young Nazi boyfriend, who says his parents left nothing of value in the apartment. He tries to shoot the older thief, Socha, but the gun has no bullets. This abandoned apartment is a privileged space compared to the crowded ghetto dwelling in which the Jews will be introduced. Holland sets up a contrast, as most of the film's dramatic action will be underground and in darkness: the victims remain below while the hero is able to descend and ascend (literally as well as figuratively). Socha succeeds where Armin Mueller-Stahl's Leon in *Angry Harvest* did not—"These are my Jews," he announces when they emerge from the sewers at the end of the war—but irony coexists with redemption: the end title states that Socha was killed a few months later in a road accident. The opening prepares for the visually high-contrast sharpness in the sewers, a result of authentic illumination provided by flashlights.

The second scene introduces handheld camerawork, whose inherent nervousness is effective throughout the film, beginning with Socha's point of view in a forest: he glimpses naked Jewish women running and then being shot by the SS. Moreover, the lighting itself is expressive; for example, when a few of the Jews cannot be accommodated at a safer hiding place in the sewer, their likely death is implied by the light dimming on faces in

FIGURE 3.6 Leopold Socha (Robert Więckiewicz) in the sewer of
In Darkness

close-up. Visually, *In Darkness* is reminiscent of Wajda's *Kanał*,
as well as the final sequence of Aleksander Ford's seminal Polish
postwar drama *Border Street*. (It is perhaps even more related to
the Argentine Holocaust drama *Under the World*, where a Jewish family is as vulnerable to the natural elements as to human
cruelty.) In an interview before the world premiere of *In Darkness* at the Telluride Film Festival in Colorado, Holland said, "I
saw Ford's film as a child, and didn't remember the sewers.
Wajda's film is the necessary reference when shooting this kind
of movie. I watched it several times during the prep. But we were
working in color rather than black-and-white, and the mise-
en-scene was very different. We needed real darkness, and I
wanted to avoid the backlights coming from the tunnels."[10]
    There is a relative absence of music, as the images carry the
emotional weight. Occasional diegetic music works contrapun-
tally, such as a Viennese waltz at the Janowska concentration
camp, which turns out to be played by a prisoners' orchestra.
Holland acknowledged, "With Antoni Komasa-Lazarkiewicz,

my composer, we knew just after the first cut was done that this movie doesn't need music to pump up the emotions or the tension. At the beginning, we were even thinking not to use music at all. Then Antoni came up with the idea of using the song from Henry Purcell's 'Dido and Aeneas,' and one line of the music is building up to this moment."[11]

Unlike other Holocaust films, Holland's drama contains a surprising frankness about daily life—the Jews are flawed rather than virtuous—including sex: since the action is far from concentration camps, lovemaking is presented matter-of-factly throughout. Poldek gets into bed with his wife and makes love while their daughter sleeps in the next bed; Janek, one of the Jews hidden in the sewer, has sex with his mistress despite their dank quarters and lack of privacy. (Among women directors Holland's films have a particularly hard edge, a result—or perhaps cause—of her work on a variety of male-themed HBO series.)

The postwar Polish cinema is one of the richest in film history, boasting such directors as Krzysztof Kieślowski, Krzysztof Zanussi, Roman Polanski, and Wajda. In this context, Holland occupies a place somewhere between Wajda—whose spiritual faith illuminates films such as *Katyn* (2007)—and the more darkly ironic Polanski (whose Oscar-winning Holocaust tale *The Pianist* is less concerned with salvation than survival). It is understandable that Polish filmmakers return to true stories of World War II: what better historical era in which to explore the possibilities and limitations of heroism? "My goal was not to accuse or to show as innocent any nation," Holland said in Telluride. "I wanted to show how thin is the line between good and evil in the human soul."

Holland and Campion take their time to establish the manifold tensions their films will explore. With openings that invite

a gaze sharply attuned to nuances of light and dark—or the revealed and the hidden—they build on the long-take style developed by Welles, Altman, and Herzog. While poetically packing
the frame, these directors suggest that—from mise-en-scène to
the human psyche—there is more than meets the eye.

4

Narrative Between
the Frames
Montage

---

*Z; Hiroshima, mon amour; Seven Beauties; Schindler's
List; Three Colors: Red; The Shipping News; Shine*

One of the most famous extended openings of
movie history is in *2001: A Space Odyssey* (1968):
an ape from the Paleolithic era hurls a bone into
the sky after using it to attack an aggressor. As it twirls down in
slow motion, director Stanley Kubrick cuts to a spaceship hur-
tling through space. His match cut crystallizes the power of editing to create provocative counterpoints (much like the work of
Sergei Eisenstein in the 1920s). Although the greatest motion
pictures combine expressive editing with the richness inherent
in frames, montage is often the key element in storytelling.
This is true of the riveting opening juxtapositions of such master
directors as Costa-Gavras (*Z*), Alain Resnais (*Hiroshima, mon
amour*), Lina Wertmüller (*Seven Beauties*), and Steven Spielberg
(*Schindler's List*), who grapple with European history. Montage also shapes the openings that introduce a rich psychological

landscape, such as Krzysztof Kieślowski's *Three Colors: Red*, Lasse Hallström's *Shipping News*, and Scott Hicks's *Shine*.

Editing is perhaps most crucial to political thrillers, whose rapid rhythm propels the momentum of investigation. The staccato editing of Costa-Gavras's *Z* (1969), an Algerian-French coproduction based on real events, led to the film's critical as well as commercial success (and probably influenced the montage in *The French Connection* two years later). The first foreign-language movie to be named best picture by the New York Film Critics Circle, *Z* was also the first non-English-language film nominated for the best-picture Oscar since Jean Renoir's unforgettable *Grand Illusion* in 1938. (*Z* won the Academy Award for Best Foreign-Language Film, as well as a second Oscar for editing.) Costa-Gavras cowrote the screenplay with Jorge Semprún, based on the 1966 novel of the same name by Vassilis Vassilikos. The Paris-based, Greek-born director gave bold cinematic form to the true story of pacifist and social democrat Grigoris Lambrakis, including the investigation that followed his May 1963 assassination. But *Z*, which was made in French in the aftermath of the Greek military coup of 1967, never identifies its geographical setting.

The film opens with hazy circular lights that come into focus, revealing a military ornament, followed by rapid shots of other symbolic pins—including Christian images—that seem to blend right-wing and religious iconography. The robust score of Mikis Theodorakis contributes to the escalating sense of urgency during the credits, culminating in the printed words "Any similarity to persons or events is deliberate"—signed Jorge Semprún and Costa-Gavras—which defiantly undercut the disclaimer that usually appears in movies. In the first scene a male official lectures an audience about how to eradicate a fungus, beginning with vineyards, before elaborating on the ideological virus they perceive from the Left. After he introduces the head of the police, extreme close-ups present isolated details like a man's watch or a toothpick in a mouth: as with the first shots, this kaleidoscopic approach invites the viewer to actively piece the fragments together. This places us metaphorically in the perspective of the investigator even before we meet him: we must be attentive to detail, skeptical, and then capable of seeing the larger picture. Given the film's incorporation of flashbacks as well, Z builds a cumulative sense of inevitability that the truth will emerge. It captures a particularly dramatic moment in history that linked Europe and the United States—the upheavals of 1968. One can feel the galvanizing spirit of the Prague Spring, where resisters battled the Soviet invasion; the Paris streets where workers and students demonstrated together; the Cannes Film Festival shut down by directors (including Costa-Gavras alongside Jean-Luc Godard, François Truffaut, and Roman Polanski); riots outside the 1968 Chicago Democratic Convention; and the anti–Vietnam War protests at Columbia University as well as other campuses. At the time of the film's making and release, the right wing still controlled Greece. Z was therefore shot in Algeria, and the financing there led to its identity as the Oscar entry representing Algeria.

Part of the film's success was due to the casting of Yves Montand—the renowned actor and singer already associated with progressive causes—in the crucial role of the deputy marked for assassination. And for his performance as the scrupulous investigating judge, Jean-Louis Trintignant (who would go on to star in *The Conformist* and *Three Colors: Red*) won the Best Actor Award at the Cannes Film Festival. His character was based on Christos Sartzetakis, the prosecutor of the real Lambrakis assassins. Finally, the film's producer Jacques Perrin plays the engaging photojournalist whose smart snooping helps to topple the generals responsible for the cover-up. The penultimate scene, in which typewriters in close-up tap out the indictments of top junta officials, would be echoed in *All the President's Men.* But unlike Alan J. Pakula's film, *Z* does not end on a triumphant note: a lengthy, sobering list of all that was banned includes Sophocles, the Beatles, Sartre, freedom of the press, popular music (notably that of Theodorakis, whose score pulsates in the background), and the letter *Z*, "which means *He Lives* in ancient Greek," according to the film. In an interview decades after the film's release, Costa-Gavras articulated his commendable goals (which are equally applicable to his subsequent films, such as *State of Siege*, *Missing*, and *The Music Box*): "Cinema is about seducing an audience to have them go away and think . . . the ancient Greek expression 'to guide the soul.' I think the role of entertainment is to do that."[1]

If guiding the soul requires lucidity on the part of creators as well as spectators, *Hiroshima, mon amour* provides an exquisite example of montage that both complicates and clarifies. In Alain Resnais's 1959 masterpiece the actress played by Emmanuelle Riva says, "The art of seeing well has to be learned," a line addressed to the viewer as well. For his first fictional feature, the director of the seminal short *Night and Fog* exploits cinematic language to teach us to see memory. This includes a tracking camera, the counterpoint of lyrical music with lacerating image, and the dislocation of montage. *Hiroshima, mon amour* explores how the past conditions—or painfully withdraws itself from—the present. He makes us see beyond chronological time, immediate space, and traditional verbal language into the realm of emotional fluidity. The stream of consciousness depicts an intense subjectivity, especially through exceedingly brief flash cuts of the female protagonist's past.

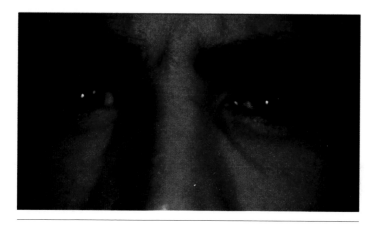

Travis (Robert De Niro) in *Taxi Driver*

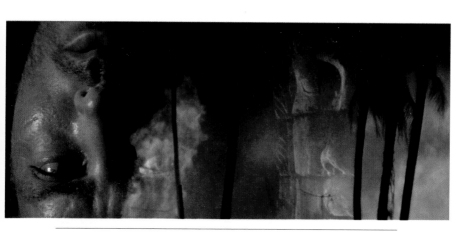

The superimpositions that open *Apocalypse Now*

From the opening of *Where Do We Go Now?*

Eddie (Cary-Hiroyuki Tagawa) in the opening of *Rising Sun*

The film originated as a project for a documentary on the atom bomb. Resnais admired the novels of Marguerite Duras and suggested that she place a love story in the context of the bomb. Through parallel montage, he would juxtapose a love story in postwar Hiroshima with an event from 1944, and he asked her for a libretto to be set in images. The opening is purposefully ambiguous, forcing us to question what we see, what we hear, and what might be the relationship between the two. The scene fades in and out of fragmentary but formally rhyming shots that seem to frame parts of bodies. Discomfortingly, the flesh is initially overlaid with sand or ash, then glitter, and finally beads of perspiration.

The voice of the French actress (Riva) insists that she saw everything in Hiroshima; the voice of the Japanese man replies that she saw nothing. Duras called this first conversation "an

FIGURE 4.1 The abstracted bodies in the opening of *Hiroshima, mon amour*

operatic exchange," as it is impossible to talk about Hiroshima.[2] When the actress speaks and the camera tracks down the hospital corridor, there are people in the doorway. When the Japanese man (Eiji Okada) speaks, the same tracking movement reveals an empty hallway. It becomes apparent through the images that she has visited the reconstructions of Hiroshima: what she saw is a representation of suffering rather than the actuality. Fellow French New Wave director Éric Rohmer called Resnais a cubist, because he reconstitutes reality after fragmenting it. The effect is one of opposition, but also of a deeper unity in which past and present, love and war, individual and cosmic, feed on each other. Indeed, Pablo Picasso's perspective can be applied to *Hiroshima, mon amour*: "Through art we express our conception of what nature is not. . . . And from the point of view of art there are no concrete or abstract forms, but only forms which are more or less convincing lies. That those lies are necessary to our mental selves is beyond any doubt, as it is through them that we form our aesthetic point of view."[3]

The soundtrack is predicated on repetition and tension. Unfortunately, the subtitles cannot convey the incantatory quality of the woman's voice repeating in French "quatre fois à Hiroshima" (four times in Hiroshima), or "faute d'autre chose" (for lack of anything else). There is a counterpoint between what we see and hear. About the soundtrack of both this film and *Night and Fog*, Resnais proposed, "The more violent the images, the gentler the music." The delicate melody on piano of Giovanni Fusco's score keeps the opening images bearable and then shifts to honky-tonk music with shots of the museum. When the actress speaks of Hiroshima after the bomb as being blanketed with flowers, we see an eye being removed. She tries to convince the Japanese man that she saw horrors, but the context turns out to be a bed, an erotic locus for a man and woman who met only hours before. About this first scene, Jean-Luc Godard found something amoral in using the same close-up to show love and horror; however, this yoking is part of Resnais's vision: "The entire film was to be built on contradiction—that of forgetfulness, at once essential and terrifying," he said.[4] And he boldly explored the contradiction of a singular love story against the collective backdrop of atomic war.

The stream of consciousness expressed by Resnais's flashback structure influenced countless filmmakers all over the world, especially in its depiction of involuntary memory. One of the richest examples is *The Pawnbroker*, directed by Sidney Lumet four years after *Hiroshima, mon amour*. In telling the story of a Holocaust survivor in Harlem, brilliantly incarnated by Rod Steiger, this independent American drama made the wartime past a palpable intrusion into the protagonist's present and expressed his dissociation from those around him.[5] When Lina Wertmüller made *Seven Beauties* ten years later, her opening proclaimed an even more audacious dislocation via montage, especially the counterpoint between sound and image. In this controversial black comedy, she juxtaposes archival footage of World War II with a popular song of the mid-1970s: a still of Mussolini shaking hands with Hitler is crosscut with bombs. At first we hear only jazz saxophone, before "Oh yeah" punctuates the historical images—a phrase that can mean many things, from approval to cynicism. These boldly satirical counterpoints are reminiscent of the end of *Dr. Strangelove*, where Kubrick ironically juxtaposes the image of an atomic bomb's mushroom cloud with the song "We'll Meet Again." The opening song in *Seven Beauties*, "Quelli che," is by Enzo Jannacci, who is credited with the film's soundtrack. He was a cardiologist as well as an Italian singer-songwriter, actor, and stand-up comedian. It is his voice that we hear proclaiming sarcastically:

> The ones who don't enjoy themselves even when they laugh. Oh yeah.
> The ones who worship the corporate image not knowing that they work for someone else. Oh yeah.
> The ones who should have been shot in the cradle. Pow! Oh yeah.
> The ones who say, "Follow me to success, but kill me if I fail," so to speak. Oh yeah.

The protagonist, Pasqualino (Giancarlo Giannini), is first visible almost four minutes into the film, seeming to emerge from the archival footage. He and another Italian soldier escape wartime carnage and then peer through binoculars at Nazis murdering Jews. Their binoculars represent Wertmüller's camera—permitting sight but keeping a distance. This helpless voyeurism prepares for Pasqualino's relationship to others in an unnamed concentration camp. He is a prisoner who is made a *kapo* (a functionary with certain privileges) after seducing a grotesque female commandant (Shirley Stoler); the illusion of his power is shattered when Pasqualino is forced to shoot his friend. Most of Wertmüller's movies explore the intimate connections between sex and politics. In *Seven Beauties* she goes a step further with a story of survival that tests audience thresholds of laughter and horror. Her 1976 Oscar nomination for best director made her the first female filmmaker to earn this distinction, all the more remarkable because the film was in Italian. Like all parts of cinematic speech, the effect of montage depends on the director's vision. If Resnais used it in 1959 to address the shadow of a still palpable world war, by the mid-1970s

Wertmüller was sufficiently distanced to employ audacious editing in the service of dark irony. The fragments of the opening sequence of *Hiroshima, mon amour* ultimately cohere in the film's portrait of an actress haunted by the wartime past; those of *Seven Beauties* introduce savage buffoons of history like Hitler and Mussolini to prepare us for the cartoonlike Pasqualino.

※ ※ ※

Steven Spielberg used a less intrusive montage for the opening of his Holocaust drama *Schindler's List*, structured by visual rhymes that prepare us to understand the story. As in *All the President's Men*, the scene is enhanced by the graphic charge of typewriter keys: they attest to the importance of the word, and perhaps to the challenges inherent in adapting a nonfiction novel. Thomas Keneally's *Schindler's List* is rooted in interviews with Jewish survivors of the Holocaust who were under the protection of Oskar Schindler.[6] The book has less of a traditional dramatic arc—that is, a hero's journey—than an accumulation of testimonies. Nevertheless, Spielberg and screenwriter Steven Zaillian rose to this challenge, focusing the motion picture on the enigmatic German businessman who turned from profiteer to savior during World War II. Released in 1994, it became Spielberg's greatest critical success (earning Academy Awards for Best Picture and Best Director) and a surprising commercial hit as well. Its first few minutes brilliantly set the stage for the dramatic turns that will ensue. A hand lights a Sabbath candle, in color, as we hear the prayer in Hebrew. This image of continuity provides the frame of *Schindler's List*—survival, ritual, and celebration. The candle burns, suggesting the passage of time, and the smoke denoting its end becomes the smoke from a train; the film turns into black and white. Color—connected

FIGURE 4.2 Smoke from candle to train in *Schindler's List*

to continuity—is then suppressed until the war is over. The
film's peaceful and timeless religious opening is immediately
juxtaposed with the wartime chaos of the Cracow train station—embodied in handheld camerawork—where Jews arrive to
be herded into the ghetto. Lists of names are being typed. The
triadic introductory structure of *Schindler's List* (which will be
rhymed by the triadic concluding structure) moves from a candle to a list and finally to a man.

We do not get to see Schindler right away. Spielberg effectively presents details that suggest a mystery. First we glimpse his hands in close-up as he gets dressed, culminating in the Nazi pin on his lapel. As he enters a nightclub, the handheld camera behind his shoulder, we still do not see him fully. When the camera is finally before his face, his hand hides it partly from our view. Cinematically speaking, the director establishes that his hero reveals little, especially about his motivation. Building on the premise of Zaillian's script—in which Schindler is treated from an objective distance, through which we see only external behavior rather than rationale—neither Spielberg's direction nor Liam Neeson's performance attempts to penetrate the protagonist's enigmatic nature. This might be a drawback: after all, we want to understand why Schindler changed from an opportunistic employer of slave labor to a protector. But it is perhaps the only authentic approach: no one can really state with certainty what led this German to such nobility. The ambiguity of the character is expressed by the lighting. During the first hour, many shots present Schindler's face half in light, half in shadow—for example, as he offers Stern (Ben Kingsley) a drink for the third time. When he brings his wife, Emilie, to the nightclub, the darkness makes it hard to read his face. After his worker—a one-armed Jew—is killed by the SS, who have forced the *Schindlerjuden* to shovel snow, he complains to a Nazi official. To see half his face in shadow—at least until he makes a decisive choice—externalizes the possibly dual motive of profiteering and protecting.

Finally, the music of the opening establishes time and place. A melody provides the sound bridge from the train station to a room where a man's hands pick out clothes and accessories. We see a radio, which is playing "Gloomy Sunday," a popular (originally Hungarian) song of the 1930s that allegedly led people

to commit suicide. In the next shot, when Schindler tips a head-
waiter (played by Branko Lustig, a Holocaust survivor and one
of the film's producers), in the background are the strains of
a tango to introduce the cosmopolitan nightclub: the song is
Carlos Gardel's "Por una cabeza," composed in 1935 before the
Argentine legend's death. The diegetic music is one of Spielberg's numerous cinematic elements that transform a verbal text
into a rich audio-visual experience.

Released the same year as *Schindler's List*, Krzysztof
Kieślowski's *Three Colors: Red* explores a temporal layering less
historical than metaphysical. The third part of his masterful
trilogy invites the viewer to contemplate not only a contemporary yearning for meaningful contact but also the imperceptible connections between versions of our selves. It followed his
Double Life of Veronique, a haunting tale of two incarnations of
one woman. In *Red* a crusty retired judge (played by Jean-Louis
Trintignant) meets Valentine, a kind model played by Irène
Jacob.[7] He seems to be engineering her contact with a young
lawyer, Auguste, who lives across the street from her, a man
who increasingly seems like a younger version of the judge. The
opening sets up the thematic and stylistic terms for the rest of
this drama. Sound precedes image, as we hear a rumbling that
will turn out to be from a man's hand dialing a phone. (A second viewing makes clear that the photo by the telephone is of
Valentine, and the caller is her boyfriend, Michel.) The sound
includes rain, presaging Michel's comment, "Typical English
weather. It's pouring." The camera's exhilarating physical trajectory begins with a whip pan to the left, following the phone
wire, and then enters the filaments. It zips underwater, as we
hear distorted voices and sounds, conveying the technological
path that the human spirit must travel at the end of the twentieth century. Circular lights flash with the sound of beeping: the

line is busy. The call is placed again, and contact is made. "Re-dial" could serve as the subtitle of Kieślowski's oeuvre. The story of *Red* gives the character of the aged judge a second chance to be human, through Valentine; at the end of the trilogy, she is given a chance to escape a ferry crash and be "reborn" together with a younger incarnation of the judge.

This opening introduces numerous elements, from the phone (which will become the judge's surveillance device) to the omni-scient camera, and from crossed wires (or missed connections) to chance encounters. The cinematography by Piotr Sobociński is an integral part of the story, as *Red* is structured through inter-nal rhymes and haunting parallels. Less a linear construction than an intricate play of reflections, the third part of the *Three Colors* trilogy is punctuated by recurring images. These images include telephones, cars, flashing lights, and splashes of red, which suggest the desire for contact as well as the fear of inti-macy. The camera's elegant but deliberate movements suggest a benign surveillance. Like the judge, the camera seems to be aware of everyone simultaneously. For example, even before Valentine picks up the phone, the camera introduces Auguste in his apartment. A ringing phone leads the camera out of his place—past the red awning of the café—and into the window of Valentine's apartment. The camera waits for her: we hear her voice on the answering machine while the movement of a red rocking chair suggests her vibrating presence. When she rushes into the frame to pick up the phone, the audience is as relieved as the caller. The camera's intricate choreography, combined with the use of red, presents a world in which little has been left to chance. "Retroactive reasoning" is the term Kieślowski invoked to describe the enhanced repetition of images; as Sobociński put it, "There was no storyboard of course, just associations whose meanings must be hidden rather than disclosed. . . .

FIGURE 4.3 Valentine (Irène Jacob) in *Three Colors: Red*

Having then defined a network of subtle associations, we reversed the usual cinematic logic. Instead of omens forewarning of some future happening, we designed later scenes to show that some earlier, apparently casual events, were important to the story."[8] For example, the circular flashing bulbs of the opening set up the notion of light as movement, which will be developed throughout *Red*.

Only on a second viewing do we recognize how the color red has connected characters, scenes, and perhaps temporal dimensions. As soon as Auguste goes into the street with his dog, a red car almost hits the animal. The red cherries on Valentine's yogurt label are connected to the red ribbon on her TV antenna. The flashing red light of the opening seems to mean "Stop": the phone call can't go through because the line is busy. Red suggests the pulsating of blood in the body, a rhythm like that of telephone wires that physically transport the human spirit. Brown—the derivative of red that Sobociński visualized as the film's dominant color—is part of this associative fabric.

For example, the first shot of Auguste's apartment includes a brown-toned painting of a ballet dancer. This idealized image of female beauty in motion will be "incarnated" when Valentine arches her back in the same position during a ballet class. Ultimately, the judge and Auguste are reflections of each other, for as Kieślowski put it, "The theme of *Red* is in the conditional mood . . . what would have happened if the Judge had been born forty years later. How many better, wiser things we could have done! That's why I made this film—that maybe life can be lived better than we do." *Red* was voted best foreign film by the National Society of Film Critics as well as the New York Film Critics Circle. It earned Kieślowski an Academy Award nomination for best director (and Sobociński a nomination for best cinematographer)—a rare honor for foreign filmmakers.

While montage is often a function of hard cuts—whether imperceptible or jarring—dissolves are another crucial component of cinematic vocabulary, and they provide a haunting introduction to *The Shipping News* (2001). Directed by Lasse Hallström, this film is a tale of regeneration, from a script by Robert Nelson Jacobs adapted from Annie Proulx's novel. Early in the film, rope being twined prepares for the ancestral ropes that keep a Newfoundland house locked into the earth, as well as the narrative braiding of tales of loss that grow stronger as characters connect. Kevin Spacey incarnates Quoyle, a flawed hero, a man who is lost. The opening scene, of a little boy forced by his harsh father to swim, is deftly extended into the introduction of our protagonist: the close-up of the child underwater dissolves into an older boy, and then to the adult Quoyle at various jobs, as if he were sleeping through them. The languid fluidity crystallizes the sense that Quoyle is in suspended

FIGURE 4.4 Quoyle (Kevin Spacey) in the opening of *The Shipping News*

animation. The theme of waking up is central to *The Shipping News*—literally when Quoyle's boss (Scott Glenn) opens his eyes at his own wake, and figuratively when Quoyle takes action throughout the film. This is connected to the theme of ancestral curses, which are indeed broken by the end, allowing characters to move forward. We see Quoyle initially shaken out of his lethargy when Pedal (Cate Blanchett) runs away from a man and into Quoyle's car. The rain is significant, given that water surrounds our hero from the first shot, invoking not merely a sense of drowning but fluidity more broadly. The very nature of a film dissolve graphically conveys how identity is a slippery process rather than a fixed entity.

The opening of *Shine* (1996) provides another beautifully crafted introduction to a hero whose sense of self is elusive. Directed by Scott Hicks from a script by Jan Sardi, this Australian drama is based on the real life of David Helfgott, a gifted pianist who went from child prodigy to institutionalized eccentric and then returned to acclaim. As the film opens on a rainy night, the camera settles on his silhouette occupying the edge of the dark screen: the composition portrays how he is off-center and marginalized.[9] David (Geoffrey Rush in an Oscar-winning performance) speaks in breathless swirls—displaying a kind of logorrhea via repeated witty fragments, with the word "Oh" humorously descending five notes—and can hardly see through thick glasses obscured by raindrops. The credits unfold with slow-motion shots of David running in the rain before he stops at the window of Moby's Bar. Although they are closing for the night, he enters, invasively friendly with the staff. His words tumble out:

> Live, Sylvia, live—live and let live—that's very important isn't it? Molto, molto. But then again it's a lifelong struggle, isn't it Sylvia, Tony, to live, to survive, to survive undamaged and not destroy any living breathing creature. The point is, if you do something wrong, you can be punished for the rest of your life so I think it's a lifelong struggle; is it a lifelong struggle? Whatever you do it's a struggle, a struggle to keep your head above water and not get it chopped off.

Once he plays the bar's piano, David's talent is obvious. From this scene in the early 1980s, flashbacks reveal his story, beginning with the challenges of being the son of a tyrannical Holocaust survivor (Armin Mueller-Stahl) and suffering a mental breakdown. These flashbacks provide a musical structure appropriate to the tale of a brilliant pianist. It is not simply theme and variations, including a repetition of the opening scene in the rain; Hicks acknowledged in the press kit that *Shine* is like a concerto with three movements—exposition, development, and recapitulation.[10] He also remarked in an interview, "The character Geoffrey plays is someone who has never defined who he is, so he doesn't know where he ends and you begin. He just embraces you and flows all around you, an indefinite sort of person."[11] If we first see David soaked, tapping his fingers on the window of Moby's (which has a neon aquatic sign), liquid permeates the rest of the film; it expresses not just the flow of his music—whether gentle or torrential—but the ebb and tide of his very being.

5

Singular Point of View

The Graduate, Taxi Driver, Apocalypse Now, Come and See, Lebanon, Good Kill

---

To the question "Who am I?" a movie adds, "Through whose eyes?" leading us to discuss the use of filmic devices such as close-ups and subjective camera. These devices invite us to identify with a protagonist, especially when we see through his or her eyes. Whether in three seminal American films—*The Graduate, Taxi Driver*, and *Apocalypse Now*—or two gripping foreign films about war—*Come and See* (Russia) and *Lebanon* (Israel)—our focus is "eyedentity" or perhaps "eyedensity." Motion pictures explore characters visually, whether "Who am I?" refers to a public being or a private one. The last film in this chapter, *Good Kill*, illustrates how the use of point of view shots creates a tense juxtaposition between the coordinates on a drone site and a character's moral compass.

Given that movies reflect the time and place in which they are made, each major Hollywood genre has offered a particular kind of protagonist. As numerous scholars—notably Robert Warshow and Leo Braudy—have pointed out, the gangster and the cowboy of the western dominated the 1930s and '40s, followed by the private eye of post–World War II films like *The Big Sleep*.[1] During the Depression the gangster represented the aspirations (and dangers) of the American dream; subsequently, the westerner embodied a code of honor that often pitted the individual against the community. After 1945, heroes like Philip Marlowe or Sam Spade were investigators overcoming corruption and violence—darker aspects of human nature revealed by the war. In the 1950s *On the Waterfront* reflected the changing image of the American screen hero: the performances of Marlon Brando, James Dean, and Montgomery Clift revealed the anguished underside of the traditional screen protagonist. Only Brando survived into the 1970s, reinventing himself in films such as *Last Tango in Paris* and *The Godfather*. These movies dramatize a search for identity (particularly from the late 1960s through the 1970s)—a theme inseparable from the search for a cinematic language that expresses the quest for identity.

A few Hollywood films experimented with the camera assuming an almost claustrophobic point of view, limited to the perspective of a particular character. Although Orson Welles was not able to realize his vision of Joseph Conrad's *Heart of Darkness*—in which he would have played Marlowe while the camera incarnated Kurtz—a different Marlowe provided the source material for an entire film presented through the hero's eyes: *The Lady in the Lake*, a 1947 adaptation of Raymond Chandler's novel. Directed by and starring Robert Montgomery, the film showed events exclusively from the detective's perspective, offering more of a gimmick than a sustained dramatic exploration. The opening of *Executive Suite* (1954) is a more successful utilization of the camera locked into a character's gaze. Directed by Robert Wise from a screenplay by Ernest Lehman, it begins with employees of a corporation looking respectfully at Bullard, the person identified with the lens. As he leaves a Manhattan skyscraper office, descends in the elevator, and enters the lobby telegram office, we sense his power and control. His handwriting about impending travel is clear and strong, followed by his easy removal of a dollar from an elegant wallet. When he reaches the street, Bullard hails a taxi. Suddenly the camera keels over—the wallet flying into the gutter—as we vicariously experience his heart attack. Once Bullard is dead, the camera shifts into omniscient third-person narration: it acknowledges both the need to question perspective and the ephemerality of life.

※ ※ ※

The type of protagonist would change again when American movies came of age in the 1970s—nurtured by filmmakers including Robert Altman, John Cassavetes, Francis Ford Coppola, Roman Polanski, and Martin Scorsese—in the aftermath of the political upheavals of 1968. While film scholars tend to view 1939 as the pinnacle of American film history, I see 1974 as no less rich, boasting such titles as *The Conversation*, *The Godfather Part 2*, *Chinatown*, *A Woman Under the Influence*, *Lenny*, *The White Dawn*, *Alice Doesn't Live Here Anymore*, *The Parallax View*, *Thieves Like Us*, *California Split*, *Harry and Tonto*, and *Young Frankenstein*. That year marked the center of a sophisticated era that began in the late sixties and led up to the explosion of independent American cinema later in the seventies. In 1974 Michael Ritchie was directing *Smile*, Miloš Forman was finishing *One Flew Over the Cuckoo's Nest*, Hal Ashby was between *The Last Detail* and *Shampoo*, Arthur Penn was making *Night*

Moves, Sidney Lumet was preparing *Dog Day Afternoon*, Woody Allen was directing *Love and Death*, and Stanley Kubrick was preparing *Barry Lyndon*. Foreign cinema was no less vibrant. In 1974 Rainer Werner Fassbinder gave us *Effi Briest*, Luis Buñuel had *The Phantom of Liberty*, and François Truffaut was preparing *The Story of Adele H* and received an Oscar nomination as best director for *Day for Night*. In Poland Andrzej Wajda was directing *The Promised Land*, and Wojciech Has finished *The Hourglass Sanatorium*. In Italy Federico Fellini had just released *Amarcord*, and Bernardo Bertolucci was preparing *1900*. I heard Bertolucci propose a cogent overview of the maturation of cinema at a Cannes Film Festival symposium in 1990. He compared film to a baby born in 1895: it grew from infancy in the silent era, learned to talk during childhood, and finally entered adulthood when it became aware of itself. He saw this self-reflexive mirror stage as beginning with the French New Wave and developing through the 1960s.[2] Technological advances—such as the lightweight camera and mobile microphone—facilitated more personal, improvisational, and idiosyncratic filmmaking.

The Graduate, winner of the 1967 Academy Award for Best Picture, was Mike Nichols's second film after *Who's Afraid of Virginia Woolf?* Dustin Hoffman stars in the title role as Benjamin, a young man returning from his eastern college to California and an uncertain future. His parents' friend Mrs. Robinson (Anne Bancroft) seduces him before he falls for her daughter (Katharine Ross). The opening expresses his lack of control. The only dialogue of this introduction is a flight attendant's announcement about "beginning our descent into Los Angeles." (In the DVD commentary, Nichols said he was proud that the entire theme of the film is encompassed in the first line.)[3] The camera zooms out from Benjamin's face, a mechanical movement of the lens that flattens space, which is appropriate to his experience of returning home. The conveyor belt that carries him toward screen left externalizes his lack of agency. The grid pattern visible on the white walls behind him adds to the sense of being boxed in. Even his suitcase herded into the luggage area rhymes with Benjamin, and the sign reads, "Do they match?" The glass in the airport prepares for the glass of his aquarium, emblems of enclosure. Mike Nichols called *The Graduate* the story "of a worthy kid drowning among objects and things."[4] Therefore, water is a recurring image, from the aquarium behind his head to the swimming pool where he will later stand underwater wearing a diving suit. Since he (and we) hear only his breathing, this shot renders the Simon and Garfunkel song that opens the film, "The Sound of Silence," particularly appropriate. Although the lyrics begin, "Hello darkness, my old friend," it is the flat light of Los Angeles that surrounds Benjamin. "The Sound of Silence" expresses the character's sense of alienation and creates a rueful tone (while the SOS formed by the title is appropriate to his situation). Although the film was criticized at the time for not dealing with the political unrest of the late 1960s, perhaps Nichols's focus on Benjamin's subjectivity is what gave *The Graduate* its timeless quality.

FIGURE 5.1 Benjamin (Dustin Hoffman) in *The Graduate*

Like *The Graduate*, *Taxi Driver* portrays the disaffection of a young man immersed in his surroundings, who disdains society for its empty affluence or depravity. However, Martin Scorsese's film, set in a forbidding New York City as opposed to sunny Los Angeles, offers a darker and more unsettling portrait. His 1976 classic, from an original screenplay by Paul Schrader, stars Robert De Niro as the deeply troubled loner and cab driver Travis Bickle. The opening presents New York City from Travis's perspective (and is reminiscent of Saul Bass's title sequence for *Storm Center* [1956], especially in the abstracted close-up of eyes). The score is by Bernard Herrmann, whose film career began with Orson Welles's *Citizen Kane*—and included Alfred Hitchcock's *Psycho* and *Vertigo*, among nine collaborations with the master of suspense. In *Taxi Driver* the score alternates between a relentless percussive clanging and a lyrical saxophone melody, expressing conflicting strands of Travis's personality. The saxophone enters with the close-up of eyes, suggesting a lonely yearning for connection, following the snare drums that ominously prepare for danger. That danger is heightened by the yellow taxicab aimed at the camera before it swerves to the left. This is a nightscape of white smoke billowing against the dark sky. Our establishing shot identifies less a particular city than a limbo. All we know from the visual introduction is that this man will be our frame of reference. From his eyes darting left and right, a dissolve to a wet windshield—with unfocused lights beyond—places us within his subjectivity. The windshield is an internal frame that represents a movie screen: glass permits us to see beyond the taxi, while the wipers clarify perception. Slow motion of a rainy Times Square distorts time, while the use of a red filter for the next close-up of Travis's eyes layers space with demonic tones (and calls back to the credit sequence of

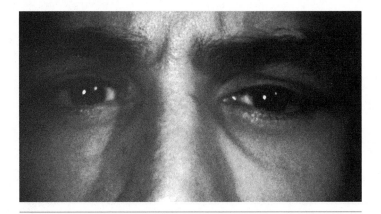

FIGURE 5.2 Travis (Robert De Niro) in *Taxi Driver*

Hitchcock's *Vertigo*). The images also contain a cumulative and encompassing elemental quality: from smoke (air plus fire), we move to rain (water) and, in this urban locale, earth (sidewalks and gutters). Travis's voice-over diary will label the streets as dirt in the moments following the end of this clip; however, the rain visually provides a possible cleansing, if a temporary one. By the end of *Taxi Driver* Travis will have attempted his own violent purification of the city through another liquid, namely blood.

If neorealism was the seminal movement in 1940s postwar Italian cinema, the cinematography of Michael Chapman in *Taxi Driver* could be called "neon-realism," an electric rendering that captures the 42nd Street of the 1970s. James Sanders, in *Celluloid Skyline: New York and the Movies*, calls Scorsese's city "an almost voluptuously lurid place, filled with old-fashioned neon signs . . . straight out of a 1940s movie—especially as reflected in the glistening rain-washed streets visible throughout the story. . . . The garish green and red light those neon signs emit, in turn, seems to bathe the entire city in a thick and ex-pressionistic gloom, completing its transformation into a fully rendered night world." He quotes Janet Maslin's review from the *New York Times*, describing "a place at once 'seductive and terrible . . . a physical manifestation of the forces tearing Travis apart.'"[5] Scorsese's opening suggests a 1940s-style film noir with a 1970s perspective, the protagonist again reflecting his particular time.

Apocalypse Now (1979) shares with *Taxi Driver* the stylized depiction of a hellish landscape—internal as well as external—of a man marked by the Vietnam War. Both include the voice-over narration of a protagonist whose mental stability is in question. Francis Ford Coppola transposed Joseph Conrad's *Heart of Darkness* to the backdrop of the Vietnam War; the focus is on Willard (played by Martin Sheen), whose mission is to find the elusive Kurtz (Marlon Brando) in the jungle. The opening is anchored by superimposition: different layers of reality exist simultaneously—external and internal—with the disorien-tation created by a face upside down as well as in slow motion. The music of The Doors is hypnotic: the song "The End" not only identifies the time of the Vietnam War but also creates a feeling of doom. Instead of a linear approach, Coppola creates internal rhymes, like Willard's face on the left and a totem on the right, or a ceiling fan and helicopter blades. These circular images introduce one of the film's motifs: *Apocalypse Now* is not simply a voyage from civilization to the primitive jungle; in addition to a journey upstream, it is also a spiraling into mad-ness. To quote Samuel Beckett's *Endgame*, "The end is in the beginning" (and he wrote that line long before Jim Morrison would sing, "This is the end . . ."). Indeed, Coppola's decision to open the film with a song that announces "This is the end" adds a temporal dimension to the circularity. Moreover, the trancelike

FIGURE 5.3 The superimpositions that open *Apocalypse Now*

experience of the opening is enhanced by Coppola's choice of fading in and out rather than cutting.

The editor and sound designer of the movie was Walter Murch, one of the most gifted film craftsmen in American cinema history. (He won the Academy Award for the sound of *Apocalypse Now.*) His skills have graced such motion pictures as *The Godfather* trilogy, *The Conversation*, *The Unbearable Lightness of Being*, and *The English Patient*, and he oversaw the reconstruction of Orson Welles's *Touch of Evil*. About *Apocalypse*'s opening scene, he said:

> You're looking at a character whose head is enveloped in flames, and then at slow-motion helicopter blades slicing through his body, superimposed upon a whirling ceiling fan, and strange sounds and music intermingling from different sources; you're probably aware you're watching a film, not an imitation of real life. Even dreams, despite their odd surreality, don't look quite like that. Inevitably, the superimposed images in 'Apocalypse Now' betray a self-consciousness because they come at the very beginning and are intended to expose and explore Willard's inner state of mind. If there had been no resonance between that

scene and the film as a whole, the opening would have been a meaningless exercise, empty virtuosity.[6]

The published screenplay *Apocalypse Now Redux* (which accompanied the 2001 release of the film's expanded version) contains not only the script by John Milius and Coppola—with narration by Michael Herr—but also a revelatory foreword by the director. He recalls sharing office space in the late 1960s with buddies Milius, George Lucas, and Carroll Ballard, who had been planning to make *Heart of Darkness*. "There was a lot of cross-fertilization going on and . . . the description of John's script-to-be included a soldier named Willard going upriver to find a renegade officer named Kurtz." By the 1970s Coppola decided to film Milius's script in the Philippines. "However, when I made the film," he writes, "instead of carrying the script, I had a little green paperback of Conrad's *Heart of Darkness* in my pocket, filled with notes and markings. I just naturally started referring to it more than the script, and step by step, the film became more surreal and reminiscent of the great Conrad novella."[7]

But let's compare the opening of the film to the first two paragraphs of Joseph Conrad's tale (published in 1899):

The *Nellie*, a cruising yawl, swung to her anchor without a flutter of the sails, and was at rest. The flood had made, the wind was nearly calm, and being bound down the river, the only thing for it was to come to and wait for the turn of the tide.

The sea-reach of the Thames stretched before us like the beginning of an interminable waterway. In the offing the sea and the sky were welded together without a joint, and in the luminous space the tanned sails of the barges drifting up with the tide seemed to stand still in red clusters of canvas sharply peaked, with gleams of varnished sprits. A haze rested on the low shores that ran out to sea in vanishing flatness. The air was dark above Gravesend, and farther back still seemed condensed into a mournful gloom, brooding motionless over the biggest, and the greatest, town on earth.[8]

This is a description in long shot of an exterior space. The perspective is that of an omniscient high-angle camera representing the point of view of a participant ("stretched before *us*") whose descriptive abilities are precise and evocative. The only words that seem to inform the visual introduction of Martin Sheen's character, on the other hand, are "haze" and "mournful gloom," while the song of The Doors provides "brooding motion." In one of the most famous scenes from *Apocalypse Now*, music again provides a simultaneous emotional tone and distancing from the action: the American helicopters over Vietnam are accompanied by "The Ride of the Valkyries," as Robert Duvall's character, Kilgore, uses Wagner's music on loudspeakers to propel his men's attack.[9] The music stops abruptly when we see Vietnamese children running from those who are out to destroy them.

The opening of *Apocalypse Now* is ultimately closer to the first paragraphs of *Dispatches*, the nonfiction book by Vietnam War correspondent Michael Herr. It is no surprise that Coppola had Herr write Willard's voice-over narration, given that the book begins with this rumination: "There was a map of Vietnam on the wall of my apartment in Saigon and some nights, coming back late to the city, I'd lie out on my bed and look at it, too tired to do anything more than just get my boots off. . . . The paper had buckled in its frame after years in the set Saigon heat, laying a kind of veil over the countries it depicted. . . . If dead ground could come back and haunt you the way dead people do, they'd have been able to mark my map CURRENT."[10]

※ ※ ※

Foregrounding subjectivity in the context of war can be both immersive and dislocating. Whether one is making a film or fighting a war, the limitations define the possibilities. One of the greatest films in this context is *Come and See* (1985), director Elem Klimov's harrowing Soviet recreation of 1943 Byelorussia. (Ales Adamovich, the film's screenwriter, had been a teen partisan in Byelorussia.) The protagonist is an adolescent witnessing his country torn apart by war: Flor (Aleksei Kravchenko, who was thirteen at the time of filming and had not acted before) joins the partisans despite his mother's plea that he stay with her to protect his little twin sisters. His experiences in a country where the Nazis destroyed over six hundred villages leave him as ravaged as the landscape: by the end of the film he looks like an old man even if only a few months have passed since the beginning. The cinematic style is breathtaking—not for the sake of self-conscious virtuosity but for a heightened storytelling appropriate to the scale of World War II. It opens with the camera placed behind an older man who yells for those hiding to come out. He turns to face the camera in close-up, the angle that will be used for each major character—an in-your-face confrontation. A little boy walking toward the camera speaks in an old man's voice—a disconcerting introduction to Flor's impending transformation—and imitates his father's exhortation to stop hiding. Flor laughs in the bushes and emerges: war is still a game. They run off together to dig in the sand for guns, as a weapon is needed to join the partisans. Pulling with the exertion required for the birth of a large animal, Flor gets

FIGURE 5.4 A boy plays at war at the beginning of *Come and See*

his rifle. After his friend playfully says "Allo, Berlin" into an abandoned phone, a reconnaissance plane flies over them. It introduces the German "Deutchland Uber Alles" anthem, which plays over the credits in counterpoint with two other aural layers—percussion and the ominous drone of the plane.

His first disappointment is mild: as a youngster, he is left behind when the partisans set out on a mission. With the beautiful young Glasha (Olga Mironova), he escapes from bombs and returns to his house. But they flee from its emptiness and from the pile of corpses Glasha glimpses outside the house while they are running away. His search for his family leads the two youngsters into a muddy swamp—both a visceral reality and a metaphor for the horrors of war into which they are being sucked. Flor is taken to a refugee camp and later hides in a village as the Nazis approach. But they round up all the inhabitants and herd them into a massive shed, to which they set fire. Hearing the screams of the dying, the Nazis applaud their work. The film's depiction of their brutality is overwhelmingly graphic. As *Washington Post* film critic Rita Kempley put it, Klimov "taps into that hallucinatory nether world of blood and mud and escalating madness that Francis Coppola found in 'Apocalypse, Now.'"[11]

When the partisans reach the Nazis, Flor—who has not fired a gun since the film's opening—finally shoots, but at a framed portrait of Hitler in a puddle. This last segment is remarkable, formally and philosophically—a kind of coda inextricable from the film's prelude. Every shot from his rifle leads to fragmented newsreel footage of Hitler and other Nazi images, including the concentration camps. Each moves to an earlier point in time, back to Kristallnacht, then to Hitler as a young man, ending on a portrait of baby Adolf. Where does evil begin? As these archival images rewind, destroyed buildings go back up, bombs ascend into planes, and crowds lower their arms from the *Heil* salute—an effect Columbia University student Simon Kessler likened to "a cancelling of history"—as Flor's cathartic act of shooting enables him to move forward.[12]

After the first bombing attack, subjective sound leads us to hear the distortions as if we were Flor, from a piercing screech to the sense of being underwater. Surreal moments abound, like his waking up on a dead cow or the Nazis leaving an old peasant lady in bed on the scorched earth of a village they burned. Flor's loss of innocence coexists with the film's acknowledgment that we are watching recreated images. At one point, Nazi officers hold a gun to his head—but only to take his picture. Once it is shot they let him go, having wanted only the image. At the end of *Come and See* Klimov suggests that images or representations can be manipulated—reversed, sped up, and fragmented—while history seems to be etched on Flor's stern face. Columbia student Patrick Ford pointed out a similar description of footage in reverse from Kurt Vonnegut's novel *Slaughterhouse-Five*, which was first published in 1969:[13]

It was a movie about American bombers in World War II and the gallant men who flew them. Seen backwards by Billy, the story went like this: American planes, full of holes and wounded men and corpses took off backwards from an airfield in England. Over France, a few German fighter planes flew at them backwards, sucked bullets and shell fragments from some of the planes and crewmen. They did the same for wrecked American bombers on the ground, and those planes flew up backwards to join the formation.

The formation flew backwards over a German city that was in flames. The bombers opened their bomb bay doors, exerted a miraculous magnetism which shrunk the fires, gathered them into cylindrical steel containers, and lifted the containers into the bellies of the planes. The containers were stored neatly in racks. The Germans below had miraculous devices of their own, which were long steel tubes. They used them to suck more fragments from the crewmen and planes. But there were still a few wounded Americans though and some of the bombers were in bad repair. Over France though, German fighters came up again, made everything and everybody as good as new.

When the bombers got back to their base, the steel cylinders were taken from the racks and shipped back to the United States of America, where factories were operating night and day, dismantling the cylinders, separating the dangerous contents into minerals. Touchingly, it was mainly women who did this work. The minerals were then shipped to specialists in remote areas. It was their business to put them into the ground, to hide them cleverly, so they would never hurt anybody ever again.

The American fliers turned in their uniforms, became high
school kids. And Hitler turned into a baby, Billy Pilgrim
supposed. That wasn't in the movie. Billy was extrapolating.
Everybody turned into a baby, and all humanity, without excep-
tion, conspired biologically to produce two perfect people named
Adam and Eve, he supposed.[14]

The exact translation of the Russian title *Idi i smotri* (from
the book of Revelation 6:1, King James version) is "Go and
look"; in either case, it includes an imperative to the spectator
to watch closely. (Unsurprisingly, László Nemes cited this film
as an inspiration for *Son of Saul*, his visceral and immersive
Oscar-winning Holocaust drama of 2015.)

In many ways, the heightened attentiveness to the natural
world makes *Come and See* a companion piece to Terrence
Malick's *Thin Red Line* (1998), as both filmmakers create a con-
tinuum between characters and their nonhuman environs during World War II. Not only are the rain and earth palpable, but
the very landscape is assaulted by bombs. If a close-up of a stork
in the woods is a reminder of the other inhabitants of the earth,
a cow in an open field becomes one of *Come and See*'s most poignant victims: after tracer bullets hit the animal repeatedly
until it falls dying, a close-up of one eye is rhymed by a falling
flare and then the moon. And the last scene of *Come and See*
includes a curious detour of the camera away from Flor's unit
marching: in a fluid movement it tracks left past trees, deep
into the heart of the woods, before rejoining the men. Along
with the gentle sound of the "Lacrimosa" from Mozart's *Requiem* on the soundtrack, this wandering lens takes us through
a piece of earth that has remained intact, still capable of suste-
nance. At this point, snow is visible on the ground, suggesting

winter (and therefore the passage of a few months' time since the film began). As all roads seem to lead to the same place, the camera's tilt to a low-angle shot of the sky suggests the spiritually evocative title of the film directed by Klimov's wife, Larissa Shepitko, *Ascent*. (She died in 1979.) Nature endures and regenerates, whether humans act nobly or destructively—a point made by another film released in 1985, Claude Lanzmann's *Shoah*: it is also anchored in landscapes that no longer reflect the wartime horrors they witnessed forty years earlier. Roger Ebert interpreted the final scene of *Come and See* as a fantasy—"The Mozart descends into the film like a deus ex machina, to lift us from its despair. We can accept it if we want, but it changes nothing. It is like an ironic taunt"[15]—but Klimov might be elevating the frame to a pantheistic vision of the universe. The last word we hear from the choral voices of Mozart's *Requiem* is "Amen."

※ ※ ※

If *Come and See* moves through varied landscapes and seasons, the time frame of *Lebanon* (2009) is twenty-four hours, and the space is within an army tank. Written and directed by Samuel Maoz, this intense and often disturbing Israeli drama—winner of the Golden Lion at the Venice Film Festival—is set in 1982 at the beginning of Israel's war with Lebanon. Its immediacy is fueled by spatial limitations: we see and hear only what the four soldiers in the Israeli tank do. The result is not only tense claustrophobia but also a self-conscious questioning of subjective camera. While the vantage point may seem initially empowering—for both the gunner Shmulik (Yoav Donat) and us—it becomes devastating, because to see through the sights of a gun is to prepare to shoot. *Lebanon* conveys a combination of heat, dirt, confusion, and fear experienced by Shmulik. The soundtrack heightens the tension by accompanying each internal camera movement with a mechanical sound: while we can see things magnified from a variety of angles, the noise of the manipulation is frightening.

The film opens on a field of wilted dandelions, as if a truck had run them over: instead of rising to the sun, they droop downward. A breeze moves them slightly as we hear atonal music consisting of pong sounds. From the yellow dandelions, an abrupt cut to a black screen allows for a printed title: "June 6, 1982, the first day of the Lebanon War." A dark circle is the appropriate introduction to the implacable enclosure of the tank. It reveals the reflection in a cistern as a soldier takes out water. A sign reads, "Men are steel. The tank is only iron." The point of view is established through a green filter on the circular lens of the tank's gunsight, moving through trees. It alternates with shaky close-ups of a soldier's face—especially his eye—against this lens. When a drop falls into the cistern that was our introductory image, we again see the reflection of a face.

Later, subjective camera is achingly visceral just after a battle in which one of the Israeli soldiers is hit. Shmulik, who was unable to fire at an oncoming car at the beginning, therefore shoots straight at another approaching one. The omnipresent whir of the stick (visually and aurally violent) conveys the inability to see the total picture. Shmulik constantly reframes—past chickens that are either in flames or wandering aimlessly before the tank—until he finds the true object of both his lens and that of the film's director: an elderly man whose arms he has blown off repeating "Peace." There are only two exterior shots—the long opening take of a field of huge dandelions and a closing shot of the tank in that field. They signify that the characters have gone in a circle: instead of advancing or progressing, these men have experienced a violent futility. The enclosure of the film resists any external explanation of the Israelis' role in Lebanon or who the real enemy is.

Lebanon is rooted in the filmmaker's own experience. A gunner like Shmulik, Maoz spent thirty days in a tank. And he did receive an order to shoot at the Arab driver of an approaching truck. He told the *Guardian*,

> "I could not escape the fact that I had pulled the trigger, that I was a kind of executioner, that I was the last person in the death link. . . . I wanted to make a film that might save a life. I took a life; now I could save a life. It's no coincidence that there have been three Israeli films about the Lebanon war in as many years [the others are the Oscar-nominated *Beaufort* and the Golden Globe-winning *Waltz With Bashir*]. When the pain is only affecting you, you can ignore it. When it's affecting your children, this is a red light." Maoz does not believe in good wars and bad wars. "War is not the last solution. War is no solution at all. War is a beast which, once released, cannot be controlled." . . .
>
> . . . "In a way, the tank is the fifth character. It's like an animal. The men are in the stomach of a wild animal."
>
> This is exactly right. In the gloom, unidentifiable liquids seep from mysterious pipes and gather on the tank's floor in foul, viscous pools. Meanwhile, as the turret swings laboriously from this direction to that, it makes a sound so raw and agonised, it could drive a man insane. This, too, is deliberate. "When we created that noise, we tried to mix the sound of a hydraulic mechanism with the sound of a wounded animal." (Point of information: the inside of the tank is not, in fact, a tank; it is the chassis of an old tractor, which two stage hands would violently shake up and down as and when Maoz required.)[16]

J. Hoberman's *Village Voice* review provides a rich context for *Lebanon*: "Maoz's cine memoir is at once political allegory and existential combat movie—Sartre's No Exit as directed by Sam Fuller," he wrote, referring to the American director of the World War II film *The Big Red One*.[17] Hoberman went on to compare *Lebanon* to the 1982 German submarine drama *Das Boot* as well as Anthony Mann's *Men in War* in highlighting its immersive experience. "Lebanon may be the movie's title," he concluded, "but, blindly plowing through everything in its path, the beleaguered tank is Israel." During the Vietnam War almost no American films were produced on the subject. By contrast, many Israeli films about war have been made in the midst of an ongoing, perpetual wartime mentality. *Lebanon*—a graphic critique of Israeli warfare—was not only allowed to be made but was supported by state funds.

We can compare *Lebanon* with *The Hurt Locker*, another war film of 2009; directed by Kathryn Bigelow, its focus is on a few American soldiers in 2004 Iraq whose job is to detonate bombs. The film's narrative strategy mirrors the soldiers' experience—fast-paced action using a handheld camera and with limited information. Both movies convey the painful chaos of war, where it is impossible to identify enemies and survival is the only goal. *The Hurt Locker* was superbly shot by Barry Ackroyd, who was also the cinematographer of *Green Zone*, directed by Paul Greengrass and starring Matt Damon: an exciting war drama made in 2010 and set in 2003 Iraq, it displays a tense style similar to the films mentioned above. In each case, the handheld camera conveys visceral incertitude while the sound design suggests an accelerated heartbeat.

Whereas those films explore the intense experience of soldiers on the ground, *Good Kill* (2015) is a superb drama that raises provocative questions about contemporary drone warfare conducted from afar, primarily through the use of subjective camera. Like the previous films of writer-director Andrew Niccol—including *Gattaca* (1997) and *Lord of War* (2005)—it moves along the fine line between the human and the mechanical, between staged manipulation and free will. Through the perspective of Tommy (Ethan Hawke), *Good Kill* addresses a particularly dangerous voyeurism—surveillance that leads to remote-control murder. The opening sequence follows titles stating that after 9/11, the US military began using UAVs (unmanned aerial vehicles, re-calling George Orwell's warnings about language that removes human consequence). "Based on actual events," the film is set in 2010. The first shot, a high angle of a sun-drenched landscape in Afghanistan, turns out to be from the point of view of a pilot on a military base in Nevada. As in *Lebanon*, we alternate be-tween what he sees through his surveillance device/weapon and extreme close-ups of his eye. There are also cuts to close shots of his mouth and the objects he controls, all in a green-grey monochrome. The fragmentary introduction of Tommy is ap-propriate: the film deals with the guilt and psychological frag-mentation experienced by a pilot for whom war has become a video game. In voice-over, he and his commander, Jack Jones (Bruce Greenwood), prepare to take the shot. As in *American Sniper* (2014), the weapon sights a woman in a chador with a child, but here she is not the enemy, and the "good kill" that follows is of a member of the Taliban in Afghanistan, courtesy of a drone manned by a pilot from a desk in a trailer. The camera moves right to a gradual reveal of Tommy only after the explo-sion. When he goes home for a barbecue with his wife (January Jones) and two children, a close-up of coals on fire rhymes visu-ally with the incendiary result of his drone attacks.

Like Jeremy Renner's character in *The Hurt Locker* or Bradley Cooper's in *American Sniper*, Tommy itches to go back into combat, far from a comfortable home life where he consumes copious amounts of vodka. New coworker Suarez (Zoë Kravitz) questions their work when they have to report to the CIA. The strikes ordered take little heed of collateral damage, including children. The film's wry moral center is commander Jack Jones: he has seen it all, acknowledging to those who work "above our theater of operation . . . we're killing people." He is a real leader, telling Tommy, "We all pulled the trigger," when the latter feels guilt for a strike after which a follow-up was immediately ordered, resulting in the deaths of the local rescuers. He adds, "They knew there would be kids killed around the Twin Towers." Jones refers to the CIA as "Christians in Action" and later says, "It's a lot easier to kill these people than to capture them." Greenwood's rich but understated delivery makes a key line resonate beyond *Good Kill*: "Don't ask me if it's a just war. It's just war."

Tommy battles his demons throughout the film, admitting about flying, "I miss the fear," and "I feel like a coward every day." Suarez is visibly affected by their increasingly cold killings too, asking, "Since when did we become Hamas?" Tommy's redeeming act is one of voyeurism turned protective rather than

FIGURE 5.5 From the opening of *Good Kill*

fatal. Because he and coworkers have seen an Afghan man rap-
ing the same woman twice in a compound, he secretly engineers a
strike on him before the rapist enters a third time. But it is horrifying to watch through his eyes as the woman moves closer to the
entrance: because of the drone's ten-second lag, it is unclear if she
will be killed as well. This rogue action gets Tommy fired. The film
ends with a high-angle shot of his car on the road to Reno, where
presumably he will make up with his estranged wife. The clicks
we hear convey that he, too, is being watched and probably not
just for potentially speeding. Niccol's implication is that we are
all being observed in one form or another. When I asked Ethan
Hawke why such a fine film was ignored—during an onstage interview at Manhattan's 92nd Street Y in March 2016—he said
the Right dismissed it as antimilitary, and the Left disliked it
because it seemed to criticize Obama's policies, resulting in the
fact that "nobody saw *Good Kill.*"

The openings of all these films invite an immediate complicity between the viewer and the flawed or morally compromised
hero. Bringing us into his singular—and often limited—point of
view, the filmmakers acknowledge the overlap between external warfare and internal battlegrounds.

6

The Collective Protagonist

While motion pictures tend to focus on a single character's trajectory, collective protagonist films utilize an intricate narrative structuring to convey interdependence. They present individuals who exist primarily in terms of a larger community: within such ensemble pieces, resolution emerges from group dynamics in a way that acknowledges the insufficiency of a single hero. Superb examples of this narrative strategy include Jean Renoir's *Rules of the Game*, William Wyler's *The Best Years of Our Lives*, King Vidor's *Our Daily Bread*, Gillo Pontecorvo's *Battle of Algiers*, Robert Altman's *Nashville*, Alan Rudolph's *Choose Me* and *Remember My Name*, Lawrence Kasdan's *The Big Chill*, Spike Lee's *Do the Right Thing*, John Sayles's *Return of the Secaucus 7* and *Matewan*, Paul Haggis's *Crash*, Paul Thomas Anderson's *Magnolia*, and Alejandro González Iñárritu's *Amores perros* and *Babel*. As with Krzysztof Kieślowski's masterful *Decalogue*, the whole is greater than the sum of its parts. Densely populated, these films express pluralism and inclusiveness. In the words of Philip Kaufman—whose own ensemble films include *The Wanderers* (1979) and *The Right Stuff* (1983)—"Living in this more collective time, we are trying to redefine the hero. We're so used to believing there's one way to confront things; but in a complex world, there are a lot of ways. It's not so clear that one person can have all forms of heroism."[1] A. O. Scott perceptively described a tenet of this kind of filmmaking in his *New York Times* review of Scandar Copti and Yaron Shani's *Ajami*: "The film has an ingenious and carefully worked-out structure. Dividing their story into chapters that are presented out of chronological order, the filmmakers embrace the multi-stranded, decentered narrative strategy that has become one of the prevalent conventions of contemporary world cinema. There are no coincidences, only hidden connections among apparently random events, some of which happen more than once so that the deeper patterns can be revealed."[2]

Among the lesser known but highly recommended collective protagonist films is *Things You Can Tell Just by Looking at Her* (2000), written and directed by Rodrigo García. The five intersecting vignettes of this Los Angeles canvas focus on compelling women—played by Glenn Close, Holly Hunter, and Cameron Diaz, among others—and explore female identity shaped by loss as well as caring for another person. This first feature by García—who previously worked as a cinematographer—uses close-ups not only for intimacy but also to give actors a chance to build emotions, fulfilling the awkward title. The East Coast counterpart is *13 Conversations About One Thing* (2002), directed by Jill Sprecher from a script she cowrote with Karen Sprecher. They intertwine the lives of New Yorkers who are dealing with guilt while searching for meaning. The film begins with quiet tension between John Turturro, playing a Columbia University physics professor, and Amy Irving as his wife. In a bar a cynical insurance man (Alan Arkin) tells cocky lawyer Matthew McConaughey a cautionary tale about a coworker who won the lottery and then lost everything. Luck becomes a major theme, as a domino-effect structure binds all the characters together.

La Ciudad (The City, 1999) is an inspirational ensemble piece written and directed by David Riker. A Spanish-language, black-and-white, neorealist depiction of life in "the city," it explores the lives of undocumented immigrants in Manhattan. All four vignettes begin in a photographic studio with a pose, a flash, and a whiteout: each episode is indeed framed, a composed snapshot that must be developed in the viewer's mind. From the beginning *La Ciudad* focuses on faces, whose authenticity makes the film seem like a documentary; however, the stylized shots and stirring music remind us of how crafted the stories are. In part 1 we see a male day laborer reading a letter from his beloved; her voice-over in Spanish then accompanies close-ups of other workers, evoking how each one might have similar affective ties in his native country. Part 2 concentrates on young Raphael, who has just arrived from Mexico and is a bit lost. He wanders into a wedding party where he is attracted to Maria, and after he walks her home, she lets him sleep on her living room couch. Raphael goes out to buy them breakfast but cannot find his way back to the apartment complex. Despite his eagerness to return to her, he is poignantly suspended in the anonymity of New York housing. In Part 3 a man with a nagging cough puts on puppet shows and cares for his little daughter. He tries to enroll her in school but is refused because they have no rent receipt or phone bill (as he cannot afford any dwelling but a car). In Part 4 Ana, who sews in a factory, learns that her six-year-old daughter is ill in her native country. Since the workers have not been paid, she is desperate. Solidarity is enacted on two levels: some of the female

FIGURE 6.1 From *La Ciudad*

workers donate to her what they have; and when the Asian-American boss tries to throw Ana out for not sewing, a potent silence grows until everyone stops working. At the end, as in the previous segments, the camera pulls back to a long shot: we contemplate the building's exterior, which hides what we normally do not see. In all four segments, no family unit is together: one person must remain in New York (like Maria), making money for the family back home. As *La Ciudad* closes with a myriad of individuals—some of whom we have not seen before—posing for the studio photographer, the scene not only ties the vignettes together but also suggests all the untold stories.

For a different kind of contemporary ensemble piece, Eric Mendelsohn's *3 Backyards* (2010) is a sparse, poetic, evocative, and riveting movie, which won the Sundance Film Festival Directing Award. Over less than twenty-four hours, three simultaneous stories unfold on Long Island, connected by mistakes, miscommunication, and missed chances. The opening shots reveal details gradually and cumulatively: with leaves in the foreground, it is hard to "read" the image (even the title is

FIGURE 6.2 Kathryn Erbe and Elias Koteas in the opening of *3 Backyards*

whited out), which prepares us to be more attentive. It is well worth the viewer's effort, as rich images, creative sound, and beautifully nuanced performances express the characters' hesitations and frustrations. The stories have simple plotlines: John (Elias Koteas) leaves for a business trip before he and his wife (Kathryn Erbe) have had a chance to talk seriously about their relationship. Christina (Rachel Resheff) steals her mother's bracelet just for a try-on but can't get it off before running for the school bus—which she misses. Peggy (Edie Falco) is flattered when a famous actress (Embeth Davidtz) asks her for a ride to the ferry. Throughout the film, foreboding details generate emotional tension. Although the tales do not intersect directly, there is coherence through the repetition of detail. Voyeurism links all three, including Peggy stealing glances at the actress in her car. The camera's narrative presence—always pushing in with quiet determination—is almost lyrically predatory. For instance, a shot begins with Christina's high-angle point of view at school before moving down and finally into the close-up of the man's hand holding her bracelet. The sound design is affecting as well: the plaintive flute at the beginning seems to be joined by a harp when Christina's story moves into the foreground (appropriate to the interweaving of a second tale), while the score becomes piercing and jangling as John drives away.

Music is a crucial bridge in connecting disparate characters, especially in an opening sequence. *Little Miss Sunshine* (2006), directed by Jonathan Dayton and Valerie Faris from Michael Arndt's Oscar-winning screenplay, provides a fine illustration, introducing six characters in separation. A young girl (Abigail Breslin) watches a TV recording of a beauty pageant and imitates the gestures of the contestant announced as the winner. A man (Greg Kinnear) talks about "winners and losers" in a motivational speech that seems to be in a big hall—but we then see just a few people clap in a classroom. A teenager (Paul Dano) pumps iron alone in his room. Oldster Alan Arkin snorts cocaine in front of a bedroom mirror. A woman (Toni Collette) talks on the phone while driving on the highway and lies about the cigarette she is smoking. A man in a wheelchair (Steve Carell) stares out a hospital window. In this truly collective introduction, the violin-based score connects individuals—each in isolation—who will turn out to belong to one family.

%% %% %%

The score also plays a primary narrative role throughout *Le Bal* (1983), a film unique in narrative construction, telling a story of transformations from 1936 to 1983 in western Europe through the single location of a dance hall. Directed by Ettore Scola, it is based on a theater piece originally created by Jean-Claude Penchenat for the Théâtre du Campagnol. The Italian filmmaker turned it into a stimulating musical motion picture with almost two dozen unnamed characters inhabiting eight time frames

FIGURE 6.3 From *Le Bal*

over half a century. While a script existed of the dialogue the characters might have spoken, the movie has no dialogue, and in this sense it reaches back even further, to silent film. The title refers not only to a ball that would take place in a dance hall but also to the shiny overhead orbs hanging in the opening shot.

The film opens with the camera tilting down from shiny disco balls to the floor. An aged bartender shuffles over to the window to close the shades and then turns on the lights. Will this space be a self-enclosed refuge from the outside world or a stylized microcosm? By the end of the film the dance hall represents both. Women enter one by one. The second woman walks toward the camera and checks her appearance; looking directly at us, she renders the lens a mirror. After the third woman assesses her reflection, a reverse-angle shot reveals the large mirror at the other end of the hall from the entrance—the locus of assessment for females who know they will be objects of a male gaze. When the men arrive in a group, they do indeed line up to look the women over. Close-ups begin to individuate the ensemble as women raise their eyes tentatively from their chairs toward possible invitations to dance. Awkwardness dominates. The looks exchanged by one couple in particular suggest not simply physical attraction but a shared past: because they seem older, the possibility of a personal history informs *Le Bal*'s overarching theme of social history. As each of the eight time frames unfolds, the characters take on a more resonant existence: rather than being lonely individuals seeking dance partners, they—like the dance hall—accumulate meaning through memory and continuity. The French song "J'attendrai" (I will wait) is merely a pop dance number in the first scene (with no lyrics), suggesting the nervous anticipation for an invitation to dance. By the fourth segment—set during the 1944 German occupation of Paris—the original rendition of this song in a female voice provides deeper historical resonance: two women dance sadly together, exchanging photos of their men, waiting for them to return from World War II.

In the opening sequence, as the provisional partners begin to dance in couples, many seem mismatched. Tensions emerge via gesture; for example, when an aggressive woman is tired of waiting for the bespectacled man hovering beside her to make his move, she stands up and lifts her arms in dance pose so that he approaches. It is appropriate that one of the songs is "Et maintenant?" (known as "What Now, My Love?" in English), as most of the characters hesitate to make a move. A burst of white steam from the bar's espresso machine leads us to 1936, where the same music continues with different orchestration (primarily accordion). The bartender is now young, serving red wine rather than cocktails. The sepia-toned evocation of the Popular Front makes the characters more attractive because they are stylized, distanced by aesthetic convention in a more harmonious world. This sequence even includes a Jean Gabin look-alike, a tough guy who attracts the ladies. When all the characters dance in a circle, they embody solidarity. Even the tall awkward man who could not get a dance partner in the first sequence obtains a kiss in the middle of the circle. The scene brings to mind a remark by Whit Stillman (the director of ensemble pieces like *Metropolitan* and *Barcelona*), "When we're nostalgic about the past, it's for when life was in groups, before the split into isolated life."[3] Toward the end, when a man in a Fascist uniform enters atop the steps of the hall and orders the band to stop playing, dance represents defiance: with a glare, one woman begins stomping, followed by the loud steps of the others resounding on the dance floor. Their rhythmic resistance evokes a Spanish expression, "Que me quiten lo bailado" (Let them try to take away what I've danced!).

A freeze-frame becomes a still photo hanging on the wall. The film's third section is set in 1940, when the dance hall provides shelter during a wartime air raid. Instead of music there are sirens and bombs; unable to dance, people clutch one another in fear. After the all-clear signal, the bartender takes pity on a female violinist: as a record plays a popular Italian song (Vittorio De Sica's "Parlami d'amore Mariù"), he cooks her spaghetti, which she devours. The following segment continues with the German occupation of Paris. In 1944 two women dance to the radio's rendition of "J'attendrai" as well as "We're Going to Hang Out the Washing on the Siegfried Line." When a shady collaborator brings a Gestapo officer to the hall, the music changes to "Lili Marleen." Each woman refuses to dance with the German, leaving the collaborator to hold out his arms to the "guest." Ironically enough, the two men dance a tango perfectly in step, the French Fascist following every move of the Nazi. As distant church bells suggest the end of the occupation, women revolve around the male couple; joined by others, they become a large circle—not simply of entrapment, but wholeness and unity.

Similarly, in the next sequence—set during the liberation—dance expresses both celebration and political retribution: after the collaborator sneaks into their circle, they refuse to let him out. A paso doble is then interrupted by the return of a one-legged soldier: helped by his female partner, even he dances again. And when two men ask the same woman onto the floor, in a moment of touching inclusiveness she accepts both and all three dance together.

Another freeze-frame that leads to a hanging photo above the bar takes us into the sixth sequence—a postwar era where foreign influences occupy an increasing role. The actor playing outsiders to the dance hall establishes continuity: once a Fascist collaborator who brought in a Nazi during the war, he is now a black marketer escorting American soldiers in 1945. (Moreover, the Gestapo officer was played by the awkward beanstalk who could not get a dance partner in the opening sequence: it makes sense that this unwanted man would require a uniform to stand up straight and give orders.) The bartender is suddenly supplied with Coca-Cola (which Ettore Scola pungently referred to as "gastronomic colonialism" when I interviewed him in 1984).[4] The couples trying to dance the jitterbug flail about, exhibiting none of their prewar grace. By 1956, labeled in the end credits as "From the Algerian War to rock and roll," a carioca provides the backdrop for racism as well as the invasion of leather-jacketed hoodlums. A thug in dark glasses assaults a sympathetic, dark-skinned man while the band cheerfully plays a Latin-inspired song (ironically the kind of music that might have been appropriated by white Americans from black and Latino artists).

The penultimate segment, in May 1968, begins with the sound of sirens from the street as wounded protesters break into the abandoned hall. As we hear snippets on the radio of rallies from around the world, the space again becomes a shelter. This is the only time a handheld camera is used, corresponding to Scola's perception, "A short eruption of hope, as '68 was." The Beatles' song "Michelle" is the bridge from 1968 to the film's present: rather than a cut, the fluid movement of our older couple brings the film back to the opening sequence. Back in 1983, one woman removes her wig and dances more comfortably, as if suddenly liberated. Even if the characters don't have names, their faces are more recognizable and seem to have a richer history than in the film's introduction. This is especially true of the couple that is no longer young (played by the same actors who were youthfully in love in 1936): they have difficulty parting, and before the man leaves, his wedding ring is noticeable.

A solo trumpet playing the yearning melody of composer Vladimir Cosma's "Le Bal" theme suggests the return of isolation as the characters file out of the hall. Except for a man giving a woman his card, there is little sense of future contact. The last action belongs to the sight-impaired wallflower who always sat in the corner seeming to read movie magazines: she jumps up at the touch of a man—assuming an invitation to dance—only to find the aged bartender indicating that it is time to close up.

Scola presents a vision that embraces history: the hall's past proves more vibrant than its present, in which couples disintegrate and men dance alone narcissistically. While the director insisted that he did not miss "the good old days," he praised past manifestations "of the collective spirit that must be maintained." The film seems to be asking whether partners are even necessary in this new world. And is community possible? (If the 1970s were a period of increasing depersonalization, egotism, and loneliness, today the dance hall's patrons might be listening to their own iPhones in even greater isolation.) On the one hand, the reflecting balls of the opening and closing sequences crystallize gaudy repetition rather than forward movement or change. On the other hand—and even if the film's action ends on a note of disappointment—the closing credits imply a more upbeat vision: suddenly, all the characters are dancing again, as if they have returned to the hall. Has the film depicted a present tense of one singular evening, or does the closing coda indicate the iterative mode? Do the characters return weekly to such a dance hall in the early 1980s? Rather than being strangers to each other, are they participants in an ongoing spectacle? If the characters do share a past, perhaps their weekly pleasure is comforting rather than depressing. Scola told me, "I'm sure they'll return the following Saturday to the same place. The end is not only a curtain call, but a reminder that they will come back next week, next year, next century, keeping their right to hope."[5]

Day for Night shares with *Le Bal* unity of place (in this case, a movie set), nostalgia, and a concern with creating a community that has a shared goal. François Truffaut's now classic 1973 film celebrates the process of filmmaking as well as the myriad individuals engaged in such a collective enterprise. From the opening credit sequence, it is unabashedly enamored of what transpires behind the camera. The title (in French, *La Nuit américaine*) refers to the filter by which night scenes can be filmed during the day—an artifice that provides an illusion of reality—and throughout *Day for Night* we see the fluid relationship between art and experience, or their interdependence.[6] It presents the making of the film "Meet Pamela," a rather trite melodrama starring Alphonse (Jean-Pierre Léaud) as the son of Alexandre (Jean-Pierre Aumont) and Severine (Valentina Cortese). When Alphonse brings home his new bride, Pamela—played by Julie (Jacqueline Bisset)—his father falls in love with her and they run off together. *Day for Night* uses "Meet Pamela" as an excuse to explore the shoot, during which Alphonse worries about the fidelity of his girlfriend, Liliane; Julie is recovering from a nervous breakdown; Alexandre goes daily to the airport in anticipation of a lover's arrival; and loyal assistant Joelle (Nathalie Baye) keeps things smoothly on course. Adding to the film's self-reflexivity, Truffaut plays the director, Ferrand.

The opening credit sequence foregrounds Georges Delerue's score, as we hear the orchestra tuning up and the composer instructing, "Let's all be quiet and play well." On the left side of the dark screen, two optical sound waves modulate, providing a graphic representation of the soundtrack. "No sentimentality," Delerue adds in conducting the score, anticipating the same directions Ferrand will give his actors throughout the film. A second outer frame is the photo of silent movie stars Dorothy and Lillian Gish, on which Truffaut wrote a personal handwritten dedication of this film.

The story begins with a sunny exterior shot in the south of France. The camera tracks left along a busy Nice street, passing Alphonse emerging from the metro. It keeps moving left to find Alexandre leaving a restaurant. When the two men face each other, Alphonse raises his arm and slaps Alexandre; at that moment, Ferrand calls out, "Cut," in an abrupt close-up that almost feels like a visual slap. "It was better last time," announces the voice of the assistant director through a megaphone. If we thought we were watching the *story*, we quickly realize Truffaut's interest lies elsewhere: to begin with a take from the filming of the interior movie, "Meet Pamela," introduces his delight in process.[7] When they shoot the same scene again, this time we hear the loud instructions directed at actors and extras, which invites us into complicity with the challenges of a film shoot. By the third take we share the desired outcome of a successfully choreographed crowd around the lead main actors: from a high angle that encompasses a red crane holding the camera above the set, this take embodies the director's call for "another angle," while

Delerue's Vivaldi-inflected score ennobles the effort. This opening is playful as well as misleading, setting the stage for concerns Truffaut will develop later. After they learn that the lab
ruined this footage, the director, cast, and crew must reshoot it.
But by this point, toward the end of *Day for Night*, Alexandre
has died in a car accident, and they have to use a double. To
avoid showing the latter's face, Ferrand has Alphonse shoot him
in the back. After they add fake snow to the decor, and the scene
is shot for the fourth time, we are more aware of how everything
is staged—with compromise and with love.

Truffaut continues by showing a scene filmed multiple times
with Severine: this ebullient Italian actress is accustomed to
working with Italian directors like Fellini, whose postsyncing
of dialogue didn't require her to memorize lines. A bit tipsy
from the champagne bottle within arm's reach, Severine keeps
flubbing her lines and opening the wrong door. Firm but sympathetic, Ferrand shoots successive takes of her "Scene 36" with
Alexandre: each time, we get to see another dimension of the
shoot. The first is a long take, concentrating on the two actors.

FIGURE 6.4 François Truffaut playing the director in *Day for Night*

The second is crosscut, including the camera following Severine's movements; by the third, we see the other actors holding their breath empathetically and the crew ready to quickly set up another take. Similarly, the filming of a costume ball scene for "Meet Pamela" depends on a light bulb inside a candle created by prop man Bernard: Julie must hold it a certain way to illuminate her face in a dark space. Repetition of a take is once again an excuse for revelation of the crew's complicity: the second take of her whispered exchange with Alphonse shows their colleagues' concern for the actors as well as the successful completion of the shoot.

The opening sequence of *Day for Night* introduces the camera as a mobile narrator and participant. Since the first few minutes of the film establish a perspective from beyond the camera shooting "Meet Pamela," the act of recording is doubled. A key shot begins with a close-up of the secretary, Stacey (Alexandra Stewart), in a swimming pool. The camera pulls back as she comes out, and rises to reveal the camera of the "Meet Pamela" crew filming the scene before descending to a close-up of Ferrand in the outer "reality" of *Day for Night*. (Of course there is another layer beyond what we see, of Truffaut watching the take of the take of the take.) This provisional frame reflects the fluid nature of relationships, whether between men and women or art and life. And when Ferrand gives Julie new lines for "Meet Pamela"—almost verbatim her words to him about life— cinema clearly feeds on (and perhaps perfects) experience. Truffaut plays with and ultimately breaks down the thin borders between art and life, performing and being, filmmaking and lovemaking. *Day for Night* includes not only a street sign of the rue Jean Vigo (named for the French director of *L'Atalante* and *Zero for Conduct*) but also the actors and crew driving past signs for "Meet Pamela": with markers in the external world, the film creates its own reality.

Truffaut makes little distinction between movie star, prop master, producer, stills photographer, stunt person, production manager, and screenwriter. This could be called a democratic vision, as all the performers are given equal prominence. Whether male or female, young or mature, each is fallible—capable of behaving childishly as well as generously. Truffaut's tone is one of gentle tolerance rather than judgment.

％ ％ ％

A Separation is another exquisite example of an ensemble piece that balances the viewer's attention and sympathy among a number of characters. Asghar Farhadi's 2011 Oscar-winning drama about two families in contemporary Tehran interweaves secular as well as devout individuals, male and female, wealthy and poor. The title refers not only to a divorce proceeding but also to formal distancing devices and to a fine line between fact and fabrication. As A. O. Scott wrote about the Iranian filmmaker's fifth feature, "It is a rigorously honest movie about the difficulties of being honest, a film that tries to be truthful about the slipperiness of truth. It also sketches a portrait—perhaps an unnervingly familiar picture for American audiences—of a society divided by sex, generation, religion and class."[8]

Simin (Leila Hatami)—who wears blue jeans as well as a loose scarf over her red hair—asks the court for a divorce. She wants to leave Iran to ensure a better education for her daughter and has the necessary papers, but her husband, Nader (Peyman Moaadi), refuses to abandon his own Alzheimer's-afflicted father. The couple's daughter, Termeh (played by the director's daughter

Sarina Farhadi), cannot leave without her father's permission and chooses to stay with him when Simin moves back to her parents' home. Eventually, Nader hires devout Razieh (Sareh Bayat)—who is always accompanied by her little daughter, Somayeh—to care for his father (Ali-Asghar Shahbazi); however, when he becomes incontinent, Razieh fears that cleaning or touching him is a sin. Razieh arranges for her unemployed husband, Hojjat (Shahab Hosseini), to take this job, but because his temper keeps getting him into jail or trouble, she returns to a situation that spirals out of control. *A Separation* opens on a dark screen that is difficult to decipher: as light moves repeatedly to the right, documents are being photocopied. The perspective is from inside a xerox machine, as we hear a mechanical sound accompanying each swipe of illumination. If these passports represent one's official identity being reproduced, the rest of *A Separation* will explore how identity shifts under duress. For example, after the peaceful Nader is accused of murder, he charges Razieh with criminal neglect of his father. Farhadi introduces a self-conscious mise-en-scène, as the photocopier mimics how the camera frames, records, and creates reflections that will become the official signs of one's identity.[9]

The second scene is from the point of view of an unseen judge. A long take keeps Simin on the left and Nader on the right in sustained tension, each making a case for leaving or remaining in Iran. When Simin says she prefers that her daughter not be raised "in these circumstances," the judge questions her phrase. Rather than elaborating, she—and the film—wisely veer from political terms toward an implicit, indirect critique of the system. (In the *New Yorker* Anthony Lane succinctly called it "a democratic portrait of a theocratic world.")[10] This introduction prepares for—and rhymes with—the film's last scene, which also takes place in the judge's quarters. In a long take from the perspective of

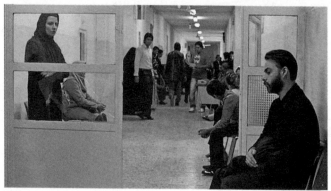

FIGURE 6.5 Leila Hatami and Peyman Moaadi from the opening
and closing scenes of *A Separation*

the magistrate, Termeh replies that she has chosen which parent
to live with but tearfully hesitates to name the person. The camera and the viewer are placed in the position of evaluating the
evidence to make a decision. After Simin and Nader leave the
room, the end credits unfold on them waiting for their daughter's
choice. Termeh's answer is never revealed. We therefore try to
interpret the lengthy, unbroken shot of Nader on the right side
of the hallway and Simin on the left, with people moving back

and forth between them. Because a glass door and a vertical bar separate her from the camera, Simin recedes into the background. Nader's physical proximity to Termeh (and to the viewer) invites the possibility that she chose to stay with her father. The film ends with the frustration of anticipation.

The visual separations in the last shot are part of the film's pattern of internal frames. In the second sequence, we share Simin's view through a window of her husband with his father, and that of Somayeh, Razieh's daughter, peering past the tinted glass of the bathroom door where her mother helps the old man. Characters often stand in doorways, which allow for only a partial perception of events. Godfrey Cheshire elaborated in *Film Comment*, "The couple's well-appointed Tehran apartment features numerous internal windows and glass partitions, enabling cinematographer Mahmoud Kalari's fluidly mobile camera to follow and constantly reframe the characters while remaining obviously cut off from them. This technique . . . sets up a visual dynamic to match the drama's emotional and moral dynamics: our perspective constantly shifts as we peer at one character and then another, trying to grasp their thoughts and motives, and work out our feelings about them."[11]

The formal strategy of visual separation expresses the film's theme of tragic misunderstanding. For example, Termeh notices from a doorway her mother counting a wad of cash for piano movers. However, she neglects to mention this to her father after he asks Termeh if she took the money. Because he never speaks of the missing cash to Simin—who clearly used this money to pay the piano movers—Nader accuses the innocent Razieh. Throughout the film, each character's situation is gradually revealed, which prevents easy judgment on the part of the viewer. Because no single person is aware of all the facts, Farhadi refuses to take sides. Simin might seem tough at the beginning when she moves out, but a close-up of her father-in-law's tight, trembling grasp of her wrist represents the hold of her domestic life. She later displays loyalty to Nader—offering to sell the house and car to post bail for him—who is a decent man, especially as a father and a son. Even the film's least sympathetic character, Hojjat, is comprehensible in his lower-class rage against the bourgeois Nader. And by the end of the film, Razieh is a victim in a different sense than we assumed: it was because a car hit her when she ran to rescue Nader's father in the street that she sought medical attention and left him tied to the bed. In the climactic penultimate scene, she refuses to swear on the Koran that Nader is responsible for her miscarriage, even if it means not getting the much-needed settlement money.

An article by Masoud Golsorkhi in the *Guardian* provides a political perspective as well:

On the other side of the class divide are Razieh . . . and her husband. . . . They provided the targets for the Shah's army and the cannon fodder that put a halt to Saddam's invasion. It's them that support Khamenei, and they are part of the bloc who voted for Ahmadinejad. Their life choices are limited to say the least. Their opportunity for flight is nil. In their world, democracy is a suspect, unaffordable luxury item. For them the investment in the revolution is an investment against the worst excesses of un-bridled capitalism.[12]

The specificity of this Iranian theocracy coexists with universal domestic situations, such as when Nader tearfully washes his ailing father in a wheelchair rather than the shower, hugging his hunched body in frustration, love, and helplessness. Like Kieślowski's *Decalogue*—which was set in late-1980s

Poland—*A Separation* constitutes a nonjudgmental observation of contemporary individuals trying to live decently while confronting confusion, compromise, and moral ambiguity. The writer-director summarized his humanist vision elegantly: "Classical tragedy was the war between good and evil. We wanted evil to be defeated and good to be victorious. But the battle in modern tragedy is between good and good. And no matter which side wins, we'll still be heartbroken."[13]

Farhadi made his next film—*The Past* (2013)—in France, exploring similar themes of intimacy, separation, and miscommunication. It begins with a windshield wiper over the titles—an appropriate opening for a film about shifting perception and how hard it is to see what lies ahead. The movie's major question is, can one build happiness on the misery of another? Its answer seems to be one that is shared by *A Separation*; namely, Jean Renoir's line as Octave in *Rules of the Game*: "There's only one terrible thing in this world, that everyone has his reasons."

※ ※ ※

Nadine Labaki's Arabic-language ensemble piece *Where Do We Go Now?* (2011) offers a fresh female perspective on sectarian violence in the Middle East. From a script that she cowrote with Thomas Bidegain, Rodney Al Haddad, and Jihad Hojeily, this fable is not only feminist and political but also humanist. It proved quite popular: after its world premiere at the Cannes Film Festival, *Where Do We Go Now?* won the People's Choice Audience Award at the 2011 Toronto Film Festival and was Lebanon's entry for the Academy Awards' Foreign-Language category. From the opening shots of an isolated mountain village, women are the focus: Christian and Muslim females dressed in black approach the camera in unified movements choreographed to mournfully vibrant music. (The score is by Khaled Mouzanar, Labaki's husband.) To the chant's percussive rhythm, the group briefly kneels or bows while walking, each woman swinging a right arm over her heart. A female voice-over accompanies the stylized and ritualistic image: "The story I tell is for all who want to hear. A tale of those who fast, a tale of those who pray, a tale of a lonely town, mines scattered all around. Caught up in a war, split to its very core. To clans with broken hearts under a burning sun, their hands stained with blood, in the name of a cross or a crescent. From this lonely place, which has chosen peace, whose history is spun of barbed wire and guns." When they reach the cemetery, the women tend to the graves of their husbands and children. This opening establishes the coexistence not only of numerous characters but also of narrative tones: just as a dance formation enlivens a funeral procession, musical numbers throughout the film distance us, suggesting a means of escape from the violent backdrop.[14]

Surrounded by landmines, Christians and Muslims live in a wary harmony. When a television is set up for everyone to watch at night, the mayor (a Christian) celebrates the transition from

FIGURE 6.6 From *Where Do We Go Now?*

the twentieth to the twenty-first century as the local priest sits beside the imam. But after a broadcast presents renewed local violence, the women sabotage the TV set, afraid the news will exacerbate tensions between their combustible men. In this world of strutting macho types on both sides—where violence erupts simply because shoes go missing from the mosque— those who suffer most are the women. Their solution is to unify by gender rather than religious faith. Labaki plays Amale, a young Christian widow whose café is the hub of the town's activity. She is attracted to Rabih (Julian Farhat), the Muslim worker painting her café: in a musical number that projects her daydream, they sing their emotions. A subsequent song accompanies the titillating Russian dancers who have been brought to the village by its women: their moves are distracting enough to allow them to infiltrate a tape recorder into the Muslim men's gathering.

An older widow, Takla (Claude Baz Moussawbaa), learns that her younger son, Nassim, was accidentally killed outside the village. Despite her grief, she tries to prevent more bloodshed by hiding it from the community, claiming he has the mumps. The film's most striking scene takes place in the church where she vents her rage at the statue of the Virgin Mary, whose face has drops of blood (from a hoax when chicken's blood was snuck into the holy water fonts). But a miraculous moment occurs after the distraught Takla leaves: the camera holds on a bloody tear that truly seems to drip down the statue's cheek. When her older son forces his way into Nassim's empty room, she does something extraordinary but plausible: Takla shoots him in the foot rather than let him inflame the men to take revenge on Muslims.

In a rather abrupt shift of tone, Labaki subsumes Takla's pathos into a colorful scene of the women baking hash cookies together in a musical number. Their agenda is to get the men sufficiently and happily incapacitated that they won't notice the women finding their buried guns to rehide them. This culminates in quite a transformation in the name of peace: the Christian women don Muslim attire and vice versa, confusing the men with prayers that indicate they adopted the opposing religion. The end of the film evokes the film's beginning, but this time men and women are unified in the walk to the cemetery, carrying the coffin of Nissim. The female voice-over (which we now recognize as that of Amale) returns: "My story is now ending for all those who were listening, of a town where peace was found while fighting continued all around. Of men who slept so deep and woke to find new peace. Of women still in black, who fought with flowers and prayers instead of guns and flares, and protected their children. Destiny then drove them to find a new way." The film's title, which appeared after the opening credits, returns verbally when the pallbearer asks, "Where do we go now?" They don't know whether to bury the young man in the Christian or Muslim section of the cemetery. Labaki leaves the question in the air, closing with the simple dedication "To our mothers," which ties back to the opening of women approaching the cemetery. Despite radical tonal shifts between scenes of bloodshed and upbeat musical performances, these very juxtapositions form part of the film's vision. *Where Do We Go Now?* invites us to take a step back and appreciate the shared, flawed humanity that can take comic as well as tragic shape.

Where Do We Go Now? is remarkably similar thematically and stylistically to another official selection of the 2011 Cannes Film Festival, *The Source*, which calls itself a fairy tale, even beginning with the words "Once Upon a Time." Starring the French-Algerian actress Leïla Bekhti as Leila, this Arabic-language film is by Radu Mihăileanu, a Romanian-born, French-based Jewish director whose previous films include the superb *Live and Become*. Like Labaki's film, *The Source* portrays the solidarity of wise, brave women in villages where male violence has ruled. It also uses musical numbers to express the characters' emotions and focuses on a beautiful young woman who has had enough of the status quo.

In the film Leila galvanizes other women to go on a "love strike" because too many have miscarried while hauling water from the distant source. In this tale that echoes Aristophanes's *Lysistrata*, she finds support in the elderly, loquacious widow "Madame Rifle" (Biyouna)—thus nicknamed because her words are like bullets—who declares there will be no sex until the men get the water piped into town. The film's opening in an unnamed contemporary Maghreb setting is gripping: close-up shots of women's feet on a rough road are crosscut with a woman giving birth in a village, while another falls as she hauls full buckets and miscarries near the source. While the town celebrates the birth, Leila sings out in despair that no baby should die. (We learn in the bathhouse, where the women are playfully sensual, that Leila lost a baby, too.)

Her husband, Sami (Saleh Bakri), is a fine and supportive mate, a teacher who praises Islamic enlightenment. At night he reads the Koran with Leila, flashlights clipped to their foreheads. Although he asks the imam to send girls to school, the spiritual leader says they are needed to do chores. At the harvest festival the women perform their strike song, mocking their lazy men and alerting females in other villages. In addition, a visiting journalist writes about their plight, which leads the government to finally take action on the request for water piping.

Even if these Arabic-language "fairy tales" seem naïve in the light of continuing violence in North Africa and the Middle East, their healing vision—rooted in female empowerment—is an audaciously refreshing antidote. They utilize the form of the ensemble piece to embody and represent communal coexistence. Their openings therefore employ different strategies from those of *Le Bal* and *Day for Night*, where the yearning for intimate connection or artistic creation dominates. *A Separation* and *Where Do We Go Now?* both begin with repetition within the frame—whether mechanical or ritualistic—and end in a kind of limbo: now that the sociopolitical fabric has been torn, can it still be repaired? They make one think of how Albert Camus revised Descartes's famous motto into "We act, therefore I am." As the African proverb cited at the end of *The Good Lie* (2013)—a splendid collective protagonist drama directed by Philippe Falardeau from a script by Margaret Nagle—puts it, "If you want to go fast, go alone. If you want to go far, go together."

7

Misdirection/Visual Narration

---

*The Hourglass Sanatorium, Before the Rain, Ajami,
Under Fire, The Conversation, Rising Sun, Psycho,
The Truman Show*

What is "misdirection"? When we sit down to watch a movie, a few questions are implicit. Who is the main character? What is the story? When and where does it take place? And why should we be watching it? Traditional motion pictures begin with an establishing shot that indicates the place, time, and identity of the protagonist. This kind of narrative clarity is appropriate in delineating focus, from *The Best Years of Our Lives* to *On the Waterfront*. But I am even more likely to practice sympathetic scholarship on the films that tweak our assumptions, replacing an establishing shot with a mobile gaze that keeps redefining focus. Motion pictures like *Under Fire*, *The Conversation*, *Rising Sun*, and *Psycho* undermine our complacency as moviegoers. They keep us actively engaged in the unfolding of the tale. Their openings make us aware not only of what is being revealed but also what remains concealed. Exploiting the resources of camera narration, they include zoom shots that draw us ineluctably into a mystery.

One of the most deftly unsettling openings can be found in *The Hourglass Sanatorium* (Poland, 1973).[1] Wojciech Has begins his adaptation of Bruno Schulz's stories with a raven's silhouette flying left in slow motion, while the camera tracks right. The camera slowly pulls back to reveal that our perspective has been through a train window framing the sky. It moves further back into an extreme low-angle perspective of the compartment's decaying decor: religious Jews are seated in a kind of mobile limbo—perhaps sleeping, perhaps dead—in the landscape of Poland between the world wars. A blind conductor awakens Josef (Jan Nowicki) to announce that the next station is his destination, the sanatorium where his father is in treatment. This opening introduces visual refrains that will be developed throughout the film. The wide-angle lens prepares for Josef's regression to a child's perspective. It is also a self-conscious reminder that we are looking up at the screen and subject to the feeling of entrapment that comes from watching the ceilings bear down on characters. The distorting lens invokes a subterranean, hellish perspective appropriate to the story (and the film ends symmetrically with a low-angle shot of a vast graveyard). The logic of dreams pervades *The Hourglass Sanatorium*, which is less a linear narrative than a composition of internal rhymes. Enhanced by dissonant sound design, meaning emerges through surreal visual and aural juxtapositions. As in his other masterpieces—including *The Noose* and *The Saragossa Manuscript*—Wojciech Has allows content to determine form: a circular structure expresses how characters are stuck in time or doomed to repetition. Later in *The Hourglass Sanatorium*, the blind conductor tells Josef, "Plain facts are chronological, lined

FIGURE 7.1 From *The Hourglass Sanatorium*

up on a thread. . . . There are sidetracks of time," invoking the possibility of temporal loops or parallel universes. At the end of the film Josef undercuts the notion of linear progress when he says about the sanatorium, "It's regurgitated time, second-hand time"—a line taken directly from Schulz's story.

Before the Rain and *Ajami* are among the most powerful films from war-ravaged countries, offering a poignant vision of characters trapped in cycles of repetition, whether determined by history or personal circumstance. Like *The Hourglass Sanatorium*, they manifest a fruitful tension between a story moving forward on a horizontal axis and a vision that spirals backward in time. (As Jean-Luc Godard famously said, a film should have a beginning, middle, and end, but not necessarily in that order.)[2] The repetition of images provides not only aesthetic coherence but also a philosophical awareness: perhaps history is not simply progress but recurrence, as still-raging wars rhyme with previous violent escalations while human needs and fears change little over centuries or national borders.

Before the Rain was the first entry from Macedonia to the Academy Awards and won the Grand Jury Prize at the 1994 Venice Film Festival. Although comparisons were made to *Pulp Fiction* (which Quentin Tarantino directed at approximately the same time), this Balkan triptych uses a fractured narrative structure in a more philosophically organic way. Writer-director Milcho Manchevski divided his first feature into three parts, "Words," "Faces," "Pictures"—also the elements of film language—manifesting a sensibility that is simultaneously literary, spiritual, and photographic. The film takes place against the backdrop of ethnic tensions between Orthodox Christian Macedonians and Muslim Albanians. In the first part, Kiril (Grégoire Colin)—a young priest who has taken a vow of silence—finds a young Albanian girl, Zamira (Labina Mitevska), hiding in his room. Zamira is being pursued by vengeful Macedonians who believe she killed one of their shepherds. Part 2 jumps to contemporary London, where photo editor Anna (Katrin Cartlidge) works with the images of war victims (which include Zamira's corpse). She is having an affair with Aleksander (Rade Šerbedžija), a Macedonian photographer who urges her to leave London with him. While she is trying to speak honestly with her husband at a restaurant, a menacing man from the Balkans opens fire, killing many patrons. Part 3 returns with Aleksander to Macedonia, where after an absence of sixteen years he learns that the Albanians are now considered enemies. He still loves Hana, the Albanian mother of Zamira. When he visits Hana at the home of her father, the stories come together. Understanding that she needs his help in protecting Zamira, he takes the girl from her captors, who are part of his own family. Just as Zamira was shot at the end of the first section by her own brother when she tried to leave with Kiril, Aleksander is shot by his cousin Zdrave when he walks away with her. She flees to the monastery, where we see Kiril in the same shot as the film's beginning: *Before the Rain* thus seems to close in a loop. Only on a second viewing do we realize that Aleksander's funeral took place in part I, where the woman crying from a distance was Anna.

Before the action begins, an epigraph is printed against a dark sky and spoken by a male off-screen voice: "With a shriek birds flee across the black sky, people are silent, my blood aches from waiting." The quotation comes from Yugoslav writer Meša Selimović's novel *Death and the Dervish* and sets the film's tone of impending violence. The opening sequence is a rich introduction to Manchevski's internal rhymes. The hands picking tomatoes from the grounds of a monastery in the mountains turn out to belong to Kiril. After he slaps his neck, killing a fly, an older priest predicts, "It's going to rain. The flies are biting." As they leave with the ripe tomatoes, a group of children play with a ring of twigs, which they set on fire around a live turtle; then they throw bullets into the circle, setting off the sounds of warfare. Even though the priest says, "Time never dies, the circle is not round," the children's game introduces a sense of violent and implacable entrapment. As Roger Ebert wrote, "The construction of Manchevski's story is intended, then, to demonstrate the futility of its ancient hatreds. There are two or three moments in the film . . . in which hatred of others is greater than love of one's own. Imagine a culture where a man would rather kill his daughter than allow her to love a man from another culture, and you will have an idea of the depth of bitterness in this film, the insane lengths to which men can be driven by belief and prejudice."[3]

Internal rhymes heighten the sense of cyclical bloodshed. *Before the Rain* begins with fingers picking tomatoes, and later a close-up of the doctor's hands delivering baby goats in part 3

FIGURE 7.2 From *Before the Rain*

accompanies his quote from *Macbeth* about hands never being cleansed of blood. An allusion to Shakespeare surfaces in each of the film's sections: *Romeo and Juliet* is the apt source for the line in the first segment, "Deny thy father's home." In part 2 Aleksander quotes from *Hamlet* in the back of a taxi, "Thus does conscience make cowards of us all." And while the priest says, "It's about time," at the beginning, Aleksander repeats these words in the last section. Zamira's first gesture—and her last before dying—is one of silence, putting her finger to her lips. Just as she appears to Kiril in his sleep, her mother Hana later seems to visit Aleksander as he sleeps. A barred shadow on his dormant face evokes Kiril's visage, which was marked in the same way in part 1.

Embodying the film's intense physicality, a character vomits in each section—Kiril, Anna, and Aleksander. The children burn a turtle in the opening sequence, and the tank of the London restaurant traps another turtle. Imprisonment is indeed expressed through circular patterns, including shots of the moon above the monastery, Anna's shower drain as well as her magnifying glass, and the two bullet holes on Aleksander's shirt that leave circles of blood at the end. Each section closes with a dead body horizontal under a tree (even the London restaurant has a bonsai plant). Manchevski's internal rhymes inform the film's structure, as the first section turns out to be a continuation of the third. (The chronological sequence is part 2, part 3, and part 1.) This enclosed universe presents a loop with minor variations, corresponding to a line spoken by Aleksander's cousin Mitre when they pursue Zamira, "It's time to collect five centuries of blood." As the director acknowledged in interviews, Balkan culture manifests the historical grip of repetition more than the Western idea of progress. *Before the Rain* offers a tragic vision of characters more likely to be killed by their own family than by the enemy. Even children seem locked into the pattern, as evidenced by the little boy (with a naked bottom) holding a gun and those who torture the turtle. Is innocence even possible? Not in a world where Zamira is presumed guilty only because the children said they saw her with the shepherd. She hardly seems capable of the murder by pitchfork that the Macedonians claim.

The graffiti on a London wall reads, "Time never dies. The circle is not round," the same words spoken by the priest in the opening. But his words at the end—"Time does not wait, and the circle is not round"—diverge just enough to suggest the possibility of an opening, a way out of the vicious cycle. In this regard, when I asked Manchevski who could logistically have taken the photos of Kiril and Zamira that end up on Anne's desk in London, he replied (in an e-mail on April 24, 2016), "They were taken by the police. There are a few policemen in some of the photos. Of course, these photos—and Kiril's (unidentified) phone call to Anne's office, looking for Aleksandar—are the two kinks in the plot. They mislead us into thinking that the story is circular, but they are also the kinks that make it impossible—like an Escher drawing."

The music is an integral component of the film's tone, which is both archaic and modern. The syncopated, percussive minor key score by "Anastasia"—three Macedonian archivists—seems to either foreshadow fatal actions in all three sections or mourn them. At other moments, diegetic music functions in a lighter fashion, as when Aleksander whistles "Raindrops Keep Falling on My Head" while riding a bicycle. The song from *Butch Cassidy and the Sundance Kid* provides an allusion to the western genre, which extends the opening sequence's homage to *The Wild Bunch*. Moreover, a shot from inside the barn as Aleksander approaches it in part 3 brings to mind *The Searchers*, which—like *Before the Rain*—is a western about honor as well as racial hatred. Manchevski confirmed in his e-mail, "Yes, the shot towards the end of the film is an homage to [John] Ford. There is something in the old west ethos (at least as seen in the mid-century westerns) that the character of Aleksander relates to. He is like the cowboy coming into the small town to dish out justice and sacrifices himself in the process."

Aleksander's final words are, "It's raining." The landscape of *Before the Rain* is indeed expressive throughout, beginning with the rumble of thunder in the opening scene and culminating in the downpour at the end. A metaphor for bloodshed, the rain descends on the Macedonians' avengers while the sky is still sunny at the monastery. But this calm is only a temporary pause before the storm.

Ajami shares with *Before the Rain* a misleading circular narrative (as well as a collective protagonist). And because the fractured chronology shows a few of the same events from different vantage points, both films lead the viewer to acknowledge the partiality of our perception. While it is impossible to generalize about the richness of recent Israeli cinema, films like *Ajami, Disengagement, Jellyfish, Policeman,* and *Lebanon* embody the search for a cinematic language appropriate to the dynamic struggles of Israeli identity in the twenty-first century. As of 2009, when *Ajami* was made, there were more than one million Arab citizens living in Israel. The film is cowritten and codirected by Scandar Copti—an Israeli Arab, who also plays the extroverted cook Binj—and Yaron Shani, who is Jewish. The setting is a neighborhood in Jaffa, a multiethnic area of Tel Aviv that has high crime and unemployment rates. In Hebrew and Arabic, the film interweaves volatile relationships between Israeli Arabs and Jews, Arab Christians and Muslims, and West Bank Palestinians and Bedouin. Unfolding in five chapters, with unannounced flashbacks, this drama makes us realize in the last two sections how little we might have understood in the first three. Five plotlines revolve around a drug deal in a garage; when the scene is presented a second time, the apparent villains—including Dando, a Jewish policeman—are humanized. And the handheld camerawork throughout the film has a nervously realistic quality, appropriate to the present tense of Israel.

Ajami opens with a hand sketching in pencil on paper. It belongs to thirteen-year-old Nasri, an Arab boy whose drawings will later chronicle the violence around him. He becomes our guide visually as well as aurally: his introductory voice-over invokes "two weeks ago," with flashbacks of revenge. He will turn out to be an unreliable narrator: like all the other characters—and the audience—he sees only one perspective. Chapter 1 focuses on his older brother, Omar, who works in the restaurant of Abu Elias. Because a rival Bedouin gang shot a neighbor—mistaking him for Omar—he seeks the help of Christian Arab

Abu Elias, who is able to broker a cease-fire, culminating in a Bedouin judge adjudicating a settlement sum of $57,000.

Nasri is not the only chronicler, as we see recorded footage of a woman in a hospital bed. This videotape is presented to Malek—a Palestinian who secretly works in Abu Elias's restaurant—as a sixteenth-birthday gift, so that he can see his mother, the woman on the tape. Her needed surgery will cost $75,000, of which the Palestinian Authority will pay one-third. In gratitude Malek plans to give a pocket watch to Abu Elias: we do not know the provenance of the watch in his plastic bag, and we learn at the very end that it belonged to a man kidnapped and murdered by Palestinian militants. He was the brother of Dando, who—upon seeing the watch in Malek's possession—assumes the worst and aims his gun at the boy in the climactic shoot-out.

In chapter 3 Arab neighbors initially spar in a friendly way with Jewish neighbor Aryeh, who complains about the noise of their sheep. But passions escalate, and he is fatally stabbed by one of the young men. As Aryeh's daughter screams, Dando gives CPR to Aryeh in vain. Earlier we see Nasri bathing his paralyzed grandfather, and Dando later gives a bath to his little daughter. One of the ways that this five-part tale retains its coherence is through such internal rhymes, especially related to brothers. (Aryeh was stabbed by the brother of Abu Elias's engaging cook, Binj. Nasri and Omar try to protect each other.)

It seems at midpoint that Dando shoots Malek—which we perceive as a heinous act—before his own story unfolds in the fourth chapter. At the very end of *Ajami* we learn that the gunshot came from thirteen-year-old Nasri, who was aiming at Dando. And Malek is clearly not the assassin of Dando's brother: from the film's beginning, violence is enacted on the wrong person (is there ever a right person?) because of misperception or mistaken identity. Similarly, we hear that cops murdered Binj, presumably because they searched his place for drugs. But when we see the actual events later, it turns out that Binj died of a drug overdose. The conclusion of Binj's story reflects how *Ajami*'s tragic events stem from misunderstanding or miscommunication.

The film's interweaving of relationships between brothers has a biblical resonance, especially given the Israeli setting of *Ajami*. In the religious history of Jews, Muslims, and Christians, the "original" brothers are the sons of Abraham—Isaac (by his wife, Sarah) and his firstborn, Ishmael (birthed by a surrogate, Sarah's Egyptian handmaiden, Hagar). While Isaac is the ancestor of the Jews, Ishmael is considered the patriarch of Muslim people. Israel's contemporary tensions concerning contested territory and rights can be traced back to the schism between these siblings: Hagar and Ishmael were exiled after Sarah—who miraculously gave birth to Isaac—assumed her child would be Abraham's sole inheritor.[4]

Ajami was a first feature for both directors, who developed the screenplay over a seven-year period. They cast nonprofessional actors—for example, a Bedouin judge as his fictional counterpart—and held workshops for almost a year, allowing actors to improvise their reactions to specific dramatic situations. The film was shot in sequence without using a traditional script. (Although the directors had a screenplay, the actors did not.) Yaron Shani recalled in an interview, "After we shot the movie, we came to the editing room with over 80 hours of footage; because the actors were improvising for the most part, we spent 14 months just editing this film."[5] As in *Before the Rain*, the vision is cyclical and despairing, focusing on how violence begets violence. Whatever their ethnicity, the characters die or lose brothers, dramatizing a waste of human potential on either side of the conflict. *Ajami* is ultimately a bracing cautionary tale. Kenneth Turan wrote in the *Los Angeles Times*, "The last thing you see in *Ajami* should be the first thing on your mind about this compelling new film from Israel. That would be the closing credits, written in both Hebrew and Arabic, separate but equal, side by side, mirroring the creative process behind this potent work and the story it has to tell."[6] Moreover, as Columbia University student Samuel Rimland proposed in an unpublished paper, "By making the tragedy of partial perspective manifest at the level of form, the filmmakers highlight the prime role played by limited knowledge in perpetuating conflict in Israel-Palestine."[7] The last line of *Ajami* is instructive: Nasri's voice-over says, "Open your eyes."

※ ※ ※

If Michelangelo Antonioni's *Blow-Up* (1966) remains the most famous cinematic exploration of how to manipulate point of view, subsequent American films—notably *Under Fire*, directed by Roger Spottiswoode, and Francis Ford Coppola's *The Conversation*—reference and embellish it, reflecting their own volatile times. "I don't take sides, I take pictures," declares the photojournalist in *Under Fire* (1983), a drama about the power of images. To what extent such objective professionalism might be possible—especially amid the turbulence of 1979 Nicaragua—is one of the many questions posed in this taut political movie. Written by Clay Frohman and Ron Shelton, it uses the background of the populist uprising against Nicaraguan dictator Anastasio Somoza to explore intervention—whether of the American government in Latin America or of a camera that can transform what it records. Nick Nolte plays Russell Price, an American who has been coolly detached from the violence around him. But in the course of the film he gets involved—with a woman, a political cause, and a moral quandary.

As *Under Fire* begins, in 1979, Russell is photographing war-torn Chad. After written titles that establish the overthrow of Somoza by Nicaraguan rebels, we see a calm field in color and hear a tense note held by strings, as well as the sounds of insects and birds. Suddenly a soldier with a rifle emerges from the earth, then another, and finally a group. An abrupt black-and-white photo freezes the image—while they don't know they are being watched, we have a privileged perspective—supported by the whir of a camera on the soundtrack. After the rebels ride out on elephants, a second still momentarily immobilizes them, then a third, before a helicopter attacks from the sky. The fourth photo, in color, precedes the introduction of Russell. *Under Fire* thus makes us aware of invisibility—whether that of the rebels who were camouflaged by the landscape, the hidden photographer, or the film viewer's status—before revealing a helicopter swooping down implacably with no human faces visible. The progression of sounds is equally gripping, from grasshoppers to a soldier's whistle, to helicopter blades whirring before the explosion unleashed by the flying object. This self-conscious opening viscerally juxtaposes shots of guns with shots of a camera that abruptly freezes—and drains of color—what it captures. Because we do not know whose furtive lens we are identifying with, the very act of filming is potentially loaded with danger. Will these images be used to harm the subjects? After all, a freeze-frame conveys the stasis of death. Should we feel guilty for potentially being complicit with a lethal lens?

The second scene addresses the difficulty of telling—much less taking—sides as Russell rides a truck filled with rebel soldiers. His old buddy Oates (Ed Harris) is part of the convoy, mistakenly

FIGURE 7.3 Russell (Nick Nolte) in a mirror in *Under Fire*, and the rebels carrying a photo of Rafael

assuming they are government troops. Although the film seems to celebrate the Chadian rebels over the corrupt dictatorship, it introduces a darker ambiguity through this American mercenary fighting on the side of the dictatorship. While Oates hides under the truck, Russell fearlessly stands to photograph an approaching plane—taking some of the same risks as the rebels in order to get the shots. Russell's vivid images end up on the cover of *Time*.

Along with his friend Alex (Gene Hackman) and Claire (Joanna Cassidy), the woman Alex loves, Russell goes to Nicaragua, where the three journalists will cover the Sandinista insurrection. This fictional tale, which alludes to real incidents, explores his transformation after seeing American troops murder civilians: the aptly named Price realizes there is a cost and consequence to his activity and places his lens in the service of the rebels.

He even stages a photo after Rafael—the leader of the revolution—is killed. In it Rafael's eyes are propped open and his corpse is seated as if he were alive. Although Rafael is physically dead, the fabricated photo reveals a different "truth"— his spirit lives. Russell's camera is initially promiscuous, taking things in rather indiscriminately, a kind of shield from direct involvement. Subsequently, the camera holds up a mirror to brutal acts. Finally it is used as a political tool. Upon finding the rebels' massacred bodies, Oates tells Russell, "No pictures please, it might look bad." The photographer asks bitterly, "Do you get paid by the body or by the hour?" He answers, "I get paid the same way as you do, pal."

When the camera is committed to intervention, it is also lethal. The sharpness of the photos Russell stages belies the ambiguity of their content. A more overtly political film than *Blow-Up*, which examines similar themes, *Under Fire* explores the capacity of the camera to both reveal and trick. The film's duplicitous images include leaflets dropped from the air—they turn out to be CIA propaganda—and Russell's manipulated image of Rafael. By the end, his photo of a journalist being shot changes the war. Spottiswoode invoked an actual incident that inspired his film: "He's a non-political character who, at the beginning of the film, hardly cares which country he's in, and gets caught into doing something for a revolution," he said about

Russell. "But it goes completely wrong: the people he tries to help get killed and, as a further irony, it's Russell's photo of a journalist being shot that changes the war—just as it was a photo of an American journalist being killed that ended the war. Carter stopped the arms shipment, refusing to send $25 million in arms, after Bill Stewart's death. . . . Perhaps you can't get involved in other people's wars. Even when our sympathetic main character takes a [staged] photo—an act of goodness so fewer people will die—it doesn't work."[8]

Like *The Year of Living Dangerously* (1982)—set in mid-1960s Indonesia under President Sukarno—the political drama of reporters in a war zone becomes an exploration of capturing images and how they relate to moral heroism. Guilt hovers in the background as the characters question the consequences of tracking a potentially dangerous story. What should a reporter do with the material once he or she cannot claim objectivity? What are the limits of stealthy voyeurism and recording? To what extent does recording an event change it? Photos can lie, of course, but (as in *Blow-Up*) they can lead to the revelation of truth—in this case murder.

If a self-conscious opening is appropriate to *Under Fire*'s concern with photojournalism, political awareness, and personal responsibility, it is crucial to the theme of surveillance in Coppola's *The Conversation* (1974). Compared to his *Godfather* trilogy and *Apocalypse Now*, its scale is modest—taking place entirely in San Francisco—but his exploration of cinematic form is even more sophisticated here. Film editor and sound designer Walter Murch—who offered insights about the inseparability of style and content in the opening sequence of *Apocalypse Now*—received an Oscar nomination for the sound of *The Conversation*, whose story is grounded in the act of recording. Arguably the greatest film ever made about surveillance, it demonstrates

Coppola's fascination with technology. This film is a powerful expression of the Watergate era, given that he was two-thirds through filming at the time of the break-in. Gene Hackman stars as skilled wiretapper Harry Caul, in a performance of impressive restraint and implosion. One of the sources for this psychological drama is a conversation Coppola had in 1966 with director Irvin Kershner, who mentioned a microphone with precise gunsights resembling a rifle. Another is *Blow-Up*, whose protagonist begins to realize that a murder was committed while he was snapping photos of a park. Only in enlarging and juxtaposing each image is he able to piece together the possibility of a fatal act.

The Conversation foregrounds sound and the role it plays in breaching privacy, inducing paranoia, or maintaining the illusion of control. In the film's opening sequence, the viewer must focus attentively while details are gradually revealed. From a high angle, the camera slowly zooms in, reframing a number of vital elements during lunch hour in a San Francisco square. A

FIGURE 7.4 The camera zooms in on Harry (Gene Hackman) in the opening of *The Conversation*

mime who is imitating pedestrians in the square introduces two themes of *The Conversation*, privacy invasion and distorted reproduction. The visual doubling he creates is heightened by the shadows cast on the pavement. (Given the increasingly crucial role played by the microphone, the mime is the only one in the square who is impervious to this surveillance device.) The second shot presents a gunsight, followed by a subjective view of a young couple. Through whose eyes are we looking? Are we identifying with the gaze of an assassin, or is the camera merely aligned with the shotgun microphone that permits surveillance? The latter interpretation will be validated by subsequent shots of men with hidden microphones tailing the young couple. Coppola thus uses misdirection to elicit a visceral as well as philosophical reaction: resisting identification with a shooter, we realize how much more information we need in order to make sense of the scene. The opening does not so much situate the viewer as unsituate us. It seems appropriate that the same word is used for what a gun and a camera (or in this case, microphone) do: shoot. Even if a film shot is obviously less lethal, Coppola explores the guilt of those who turn people into objects captured electronically. The scene culminates in the van that serves as the wiretappers' provisional headquarters, and its two-way mirror is another invasion of privacy.

The music grows louder, as do the sound effects, when the camera pans the crowd from eye level. The distorted sound of the couple's conversation alerts us to the real focus of this opening: they are the targets of aural voyeurs ("auditeurs"?) who are paid to eavesdrop on them. Later in the film Hackman's character goes to the office of the "director" (Robert Duvall). The latter is seen beside a miniature set, suggesting that he is a double for the filmmaker. His assistant (played by a young Harrison Ford) has a telescope. In retrospect, the first shot could be

FIGURE 7.5 The microphone/gun from *The Conversation*

from the perspective of the director's office. When Harry visits this office, we see the extent to which he, too, is obsessed with control. And there might be a personal resonance for Coppola if we ponder the degree of control that a film director might have. The camera of *The Conversation* is omniscient and manipulative. It is noticeably static in Harry's apartment, but when he rents a motel room adjoining the one where he fears a murder will take place—enabled by his audiotapes—the camera circles the space. At the end, it circles Harry's apartment with similar determination, suggesting that an unseen party is watching.

One of the questions Coppola raises in the film is, what can we trust? Not the tape Harry has made, which is distorted at the end. (The line, "He'd kill us if he got the chance," has a different meaning in the opening scene and at the end, depending on which word is emphasized: "He'd *kill* us" or "He'd kill *us* if he got the chance.")[9] Unlike traditional motion pictures, this one offers the unsettling reply that nothing can be trusted, not even the images and sounds created by filmmakers. *The Conversation* proposes a vigilant skepticism, as do other key films of the same year, including Roman Polanski's *Chinatown*, Bob Fosse's *Lenny*, and *The Parallax View*, directed by Alan J. Pakula (who also made *All the President's Men*).

Coppola shares with another San Francisco–based filmmaker the cinematic interrogation of what to trust as movie viewers. Philip Kaufman elaborated on this theme in his version of *Invasion of the Body Snatchers* in 1978. Whether he presents a gradual revelation or a twist in perspective, there is an inherently political component to his narrative strategy of disorientation. Because his films—including *The Right Stuff*, *The Unbearable Lightness of Being*, and *Quills*—often lead us to look more closely and critically at the images surrounding us, we see how easy it is to be duped and how vigilant a viewer—or a citizen—must remain. Likewise, his *Rising Sun* (1993) acknowledges the potential duplicity of recorded images.[10] If the focus of Michael Crichton's 1992 bestseller was a Japanese corporate takeover in the United States, Kaufman's film deftly juggles at least four strands: a murder mystery, a satire on American business confronted by Japanese investment, a mentoring relationship in which a feisty detective is paired with a mysterious sage, and an exploration of whether we can believe what we see.

In the sleek boardroom of a Los Angeles skyscraper owned by a Japanese firm, a young American woman is found dead after kinky sex with an unidentified man. Two LAPD special liaison detectives are brought in to investigate Cheryl's murder: the elegant, Japanese-speaking John Connor (Sean Connery) and Web Smith (Wesley Snipes), a volatile, divorced African-American father. The two seem to have little in common, but together they unravel the murder mystery, which is both revealed and obscured by technology. John is given a laser disc that recorded the sexual escapade and strangling in the boardroom. The killer's face is not visible, until John and Web notice a reflection that turns out to be Eddie (Cary-Hiroyuki Tagawa), Cheryl's rich boyfriend. Case closed? Not quite. Jingo, a Japanese-American computer video expert (with a deformed hand), shows them how the disc has been doctored: Eddie's face was inserted.

Beginning with the sound of Japanese taiko drums as the camera zooms into red on a black screen, the opening sequence of *Rising Sun* unsettles the viewer. Kaufman said in an e-mail, "That red in the opening is the sun, not exactly meant as symbol, more as representation: glare, intense heat, the place where our eyes are not supposed to look for fear of being blinded." A jarring human yell accompanies images of ants roasting in the sun before being crushed by horses' hooves, a dog carrying a hand, then a woman tied up on horseback. The shocking accumulation of stylized images seems to be from a western, but the camera recedes from a screen in a Karaoke club. This film within a film turns out to be the background for the song "Don't Fence Me In," sung by Eddie and four Asian-American men doing backup. The film reminds us that there is always something we are not seeing beyond the immediate frame. This opening sequence also introduces the theme of untrustworthy video images. The displacement of Cole Porter's music performed by a "yakuza" barbershop quartet offers a witty preparation for the juxtaposition of cultures that the film will explore. The hands of the woman on horseback are bound—foreshadowing the bondage we will later see in Cheryl's bed—and are then untied, appropriately enough, when we hear the lyrics "Set me loose." Moreover, the severed hand in the dog's mouth might prepare us for the deformed hand of Jingo.

As the camera moves further back, we realize just how partial our perception has been: in what seemed like a nighttime scene in an Asian city, Cheryl—fed up with Eddie's singing—gets up

FIGURE 7.6 Eddie (Cary-Hiroyuki Tagawa) in the opening of *Rising Sun*

from the bar and goes out into a brightly lit Los Angeles. As Kaufman told me in July 1993, "If Crichton said he was issuing a wake-up call to America (the economic sector) . . . the film is a wake-up call to what Americans need in film-viewing habits." A camera tilt from Cheryl's red sports car to the top of a sky-scraper tower includes the title "February 9, 6:13 A.M.": as in *Psycho*, the printed detail of time and place accompanies a voy-euristic self-awareness. If Hitchcock's film of 1960 takes us through half-closed blinds into a dark hotel room where a partly undressed woman is in bed with a man, Kaufman shifts the voy-eurism from the erotic to the technological, foregrounding the surveillance aspect we saw in *The Conversation*. As I wrote in my book about Kaufman: "When his characters engage in pleasur-able erotic activity, the camera invites our own voyeurism; but when they are captured by surveillance monitors, a discomfit-ing identification with control expresses his anti-authoritarian stance. In Kaufman's films, what voyeurism is to pleasure, sur-veillance is to control. Unlike voyeurism, surveillance denies privacy or intimacy. If the erotic gaze is strongest when shared by the subject and object, surveillance depends upon an imbalance of power between the one who controls the gaze, and its unwitting object."[11] When I asked Kaufman about the allusion to *Psycho*, he said it had not been conscious: "I wish I had intended it," he replied. "I love the idea that both films deal with voyeurism while being a murder mystery."

※ ※ ※

Alfred Hitchcock was the master not only of suspense but also of the self-conscious voyeuristic gaze, and the opening of *Psycho* constitutes a textbook case of heightened peeping. The credit sequence designed by Saul Bass provides an organic frame, introducing titles that are jagged and fragmented. Given what we later learn of Norman Bates, the titles are a graphic depiction of split personality. The verticals become the buildings of the first shot, and the horizontals become the blinds. The famous sequence establishes the camera as an active narrative presence and the audience as a group of Peeping Toms. The titles of time and place suggest the authenticity of what we now call a procedural, tracking details as if facts were verifiable. The camera moves stealthily from an establishing shot of Phoenix into a closer view, and finally through a half-closed window into darkness. This voyeuristic penetration of closed blinds reveals, appropriately enough, a couple engaged in illicit sexual activity. Like the camera, we are merely curious observers at this stage. But Hitchcock will soon lead us out of detachment and into compelling identification with ambiguous characters. (The misdirection of Hitchcock's opening includes the camera finding the film's star, Janet Leigh. He will wreak havoc with audience expectations by having her killed in the first third of the film.)

Through the gradually increasing use of subjective camera, we are first involved with Marion, a thief (Leigh), and then with Norman, a Peeping Tom (Anthony Perkins). In a probing article entitled "Hitchcock, Truffaut, and the Irresponsible Audience," Leo Braudy explains how Hitchcock is able to manipulate our sympathy for a character who will turn out to be a deranged murderer: "We follow Norman into the next room and watch as he moves aside a picture to reveal a peephole into Marion's cabin. He watches her undress and, in some important way, we feel the temptress is more guilty than the Peeping Tom. . . . Whether we realize it or not, we have had a Norman-like perspective from the beginning of the movie . . . this time, like the first time, we know we won't be caught. We tend to blame Marion and not Norman because we are fellow-voyeurs with him, and we do not want to blame ourselves."[12] Hitchcock's meticulous camera placement and movement are expressive throughout. For example, a two-shot of Norman under a stuffed bird suggests a link between the two. This is developed in a low-angle close-up of Norman's chin as he chews. He is depicted as a bird of prey, related to the slashing beaks of Hitchcock's next film, *The Birds*. By contrast, extreme high-angle shots in the old house are not only for practical reasons—we cannot see Mother's face—but also provide a bird's-eye perspective, the illusion of a privileged perch above the terror. As Lila (Vera Miles) approaches the house toward the end of the film, the forward tracking shots characteristic of *Psycho* carry her and us deeper into a literal and figurative darkness. When she enters the cellar, the moment of truth is therefore expressed by the lighting. She hits a naked bulb whose swinging intermittent light casts dizzying patterns in the dark and animates the empty sockets of Mother's eyes. On a formal level, this completes the pattern of

FIGURE 7.7   Norman (Anthony Perkins) in *Psycho*

imagery of hollow eyes, from the end of the shower sequence—
where Marion's inanimate eye rhymes visually with a drain—to
the stuffed birds, to Norman's tirade against institutions because
of "the cruel eyes studying you."

The gaze of the film's audience is presumably more benign,
the portal of a voyeurism less cruel than curious. A fascinating
(and prescient) cinematic riff in this regard is *The Truman Show*
(1998), directed by Peter Weir from an original screenplay by Andrew Niccol. This dramatic comedy invites speculation on how
free a human being can be in a society where manipulation by an
unseen force is the norm. In an ongoing TV broadcast, Truman
Burbank (Jim Carrey) is unaware that he is always on camera.
He lives in an idyllic house with a perky wife (Laura Linney),
drives to his insurance job in picture-postcard Seahaven, and
smiles broadly. The multilayered opening sequence turns out
to be as self-consciously fabricated as those of great Hollywood
predecessors like Preston Sturges's *Sullivan's Travels* (1941) and
Ernst Lubitsch's *To Be or Not to Be* (1942): in the opening scenes
of these two older films, the reality we think we are seeing

turns out to be a movie excerpt in the former and a play being rehearsed in the latter. Christof (Ed Harris) says to the camera, "We've become bored with watching actors give us phony emotions. We are tired of pyrotechnics and special effects. While the world he inhabits is, in some respects, counterfeit, there's nothing fake about Truman himself. No scripts, no cue cards. It isn't always Shakespeare, but it's genuine. It's a life." We then see Truman as the camera zooms out: he, too, directly addresses a camera, but unwittingly, as this is a private moment of doubt in his bathroom mirror: "I'm not gonna make it." An attentive viewer might notice pixilated horizontal lines as well as a green LIVE sign on the bottom right corner: in retrospect, these alert us to an external recording device. We are seeing him on a TV monitor, like the audience within the film. The credits are for the "real" Truman Show (and it is appropriately ironic that his name is a combination of *true* and *man*), "starring Truman Burbank as himself," and "created by Christof."

Interviews with the actors offer a double performance. Laura Linney plays actress Hannah Gill, who plays Meryl, the wife, and calls her role a blessed life. Noah Emmerich, as the actor Louis who plays Truman's friend Marlon, says, "Nothing here is fake. It's merely controlled." The inner frame begins with a title card, "Day 10,909," before we follow the gregarious persona that Truman projects to everyone around him. The staged reality of *The Truman Show*—which uses a genial man's daily experience as hugely popular entertainment for bored viewers—constitutes an uneasy hybrid. Truman's fans avidly watch his life broadcast around the clock. Presaging the surveillance now prevalent in streets and buildings, Weir masterfully portrays a brave new world where five thousand hidden cameras record Truman's every move. (No commercials are needed because the product placement is within the show's decor and dialogue.)

FIGURE 7.8 Truman (Jim Carrey) in *The Truman Show*

Truman believes he is the subject of his own life but is really the object of the director Christof. Once we are aware of his exploitation of Truman, do we identify with the protagonist or the puppet master? Christof's name may suggest a religious dimension, but Polish director Krzysztof Kieślowski seems more relevant: his films—notably *The Decalogue* (1989)—question whether the script of our lives is already written. In *Blind Chance* (1987) Kieślowski dramatizes the extent to which human beings are free or subject to the whims of either destiny or a capricious divinity. (The music of Wojciech Kilar, who composed the score of *Blind Chance*, is part of the soundtrack of *The Truman Show*.) Truman grows suspicious and ultimately realizes that he exists for the eyes of others. He tries to escape the island, finally making it to the edge of the set: our hero exits the frame, his freedom contingent on the audience (internal and external) letting him go. When the film critic David Thomson was in-vited by the *Guardian* in 2011 to discuss his favorite movie, he selected *The Truman Show*, lauding how "Truman finds the courage and the means to escape and that leads to one of the great moments in movie history (for me) when he and his small boat come to the point where the enormous dome protects and imprisons Seahaven—as well as his life so far and The Truman Show, the mundane epic he has been playing all his life. The dome drops down to the sea like a screen—both a movie screen and the kind of screen that prevents us from looking or going beyond a certain place. But Truman is going to go beyond it."[13] After the misdirection of the film's introduction, we too—while being entertained—have moved into a more vigorous skepticism and lucidity about viewing screen images critically.

8

Voice-Over Narration/Flashback

Sunset Boulevard, American Beauty, Fight Club, Badlands

From openings that focus on the camera's selective revelation of information, we move to the role of voice-over narration in creating as well as subverting narrative expectations. For a temporally sequential medium like the cinema, circular structures ignite a particular tension. Or as Victor Brombert wisely observed about Mircea Eliade's book *The Myth of Eternal Return*, "Our biological and cultural makeup is such that we require to fight sheer linearity (which means submission to undoing) by invoking notions of cyclical rehabilitation. . . . Modern man, according to this view, is in particular need of this rehabilitation, as he feels the anguish of his linear, progress-oriented notion of history, as well as of the inexorable laws of evolutionism. In Eliade's perspective, history and progress are perceived as a fall implying the loss of the paradise of archetypes and of repetition, and a longing for the *axis mundi* that might offer resistance to concrete historic time."[1] Films that unfold in flashback—such as *Fight Club* and *Pulp*

Fiction—embody this tension, beginning and ending with the same shot.

For a generation used to the power of literally rewinding to an earlier point, the "return" notion inherent in flashbacks is a given. Countless films begin at a moment that is actually the end of the story and then go back in time to trace how the characters and situations arrived there. The flashback structure is not merely a stylistic choice on the part of the screenwriter or director but a thematic and even philosophical one. Flashbacks make the viewer aware of time itself, and often of circularity: rewinding takes place each time the film ends—and begins again—on circular reels. Flashbacks heighten the degree to which a film is self-enclosed and foreground the self-conscious act of storytelling (including the fallible narrator). For example, *The Imitation Game* (2014) begins with Benedict Cumberbatch's voice-over asking, "Are you paying attention?" This question is directed not only at the policeman who is interrogating his character, Alan Turing, in a 1951 Manchester police station but also at the viewer. "You cannot judge me until I'm finished," he says. Flashbacks to World War II present his leadership of the secret British group that is trying to break the German Enigma code system and decipher messages. The film keeps circling back to 1951: each time we return, we know more. The concentric narration of Morten Tyldum's drama—from an Oscar-winning screenplay by Graham Moore—enables us to understand both Turing's intellectual excitement and his personal vulnerability as a gay man.

Interrupting the linear flow of the story, flashbacks are particularly appropriate for expressing the fragmentation we associate with a postmodern world. Nevertheless, this structure was already prevalent in 1940s film noir and then used cleverly by Billy Wilder in *Sunset Boulevard* (1950). What do we make of a story narrated by a man who is already dead? Wilder was a brilliant chronicler of characters less "heroic" than vain, greedy, or simply lost. Although he allegedly told his cowriter, Charles Brackett, that *Sunset Boulevard* would be a tender film about a silent movie star who makes a comeback twenty years after the world has forgotten her, their black-and-white drama turned out to be a cynical portrait of Hollywood vanity and opportunism. He cast silent-movie star Gloria Swanson as diva Norma Desmond and William Holden as Gillis, the ambitious young screenwriter who becomes her kept man. Gillis's voice-over dominates the soundtrack from the opening lines: "Yes, this is Sunset Boulevard, Los Angeles, California. It's about 5 o'clock in the morning. That's the homicide squad, complete with detectives and newspaper men." Accompanying exterior shots of a mansion, his narration purports to offer "the whole truth." But the camera aimed at a floating body from the bottom of the swimming pool is already lying. With the policemen looking down, a shot through water could never yield such clarity. (Wilder had a large mirror placed at the bottom of the pool and shot into its reflection.) This particular perspective makes us feel like we have sunk to the lowest point, perhaps appropriate to a film about far-from-noble characters. In actuality, Wilder shot the scene after the movie was completed. The original version began in a morgue, including voices of the corpses. After a preview audience laughed, he added the voice-over of Gillis and the tracking shot of the street in lieu of the morgue. His voice takes us back six months: the camera enters the window through curtains—a pre-*Psycho* penetration of the frame before the story really begins—and finds Gillis at his typewriter.

In fine film noir fashion (appropriate to the writer-director of *Double Indemnity*), *Sunset Boulevard* ends where it began. Although we have learned that the corpse floating in the swimming

FIGURE 8.1 The corpse in the swimming pool of *Sunset Boulevard*

pool is Gillis—who was shot by Norma after he rejected her—
his voice-over continues: "Well, this is where you came in, back
at that pool again, the one I always wanted. It's dawn now and
they must have photographed me a thousand times." For a film
whose riveting focus is an imperious star of silent movies,
words provide the frame. Even Norma's concluding walk down
the stairs of her mansion—amid photographers and reporters
prepared for her arrest—is accompanied by Gillis's voice beyond the grave: "So they were turning after all, those cameras.
Life, which can be strangely merciful, had taken pity on Norma
Desmond. The dream she had clung to so desperately had en-
folded her."

American Beauty adopts a similar narrative structure, told
from beyond the grave of the protagonist. Released in 1999,
Sam Mendes's Oscar-winning film, scripted by Alan Ball, is
a savagely funny critique of the suburban, consumerist family,
laced with transcendent glimmers. Kevin Spacey plays Lester, a

nonentity who barely communicates with his tightly coiled wife (Annette Bening), a real estate agent, or sullen teenage daughter, Jane (Thora Birch), whose face opens the film. He comes alive only upon seeing Jane's friend Angela (Mena Suvari), a sexy "American beauty" that he imagines covered in the eponymous rose petals of the movie's title. Although the film chronicles his transformation from wimp to aggressively hedonistic man in control, the secondary characters are sharply drawn. The family that moves next door has a shattering effect on Lester's household, especially Fitts (Chris Cooper), a colonel who tries to keep his enigmatic teenaged son, Ricky (Wes Bentley), in line. His wife, Barbara (Allison Janney), is a poignant cipher lost between an angry, gun-collecting husband and a son who secretly sells drugs to pay for his videotaping habit. Ricky is like a younger, pot-smoking version of Lester, one who manages to get away with the things for which his older neighbor yearns. After Ricky quits his catering job, Lester tells him, "You've just become my hero," and then resigns from his own employment.

Ricky is a voyeur, hiding behind his camera and taping Jane; she grows to like it, perhaps because he is the only one who really looks at her. *American Beauty* opens with the self-conscious internal frame of his gaze as Jane, lying on her side, speaks into the camera. The film plays with our voyeurism as well as our assumptions about the time frame: the first image—Jane asking Ricky to kill Lester—is later revealed to be a flash-forward. The second scene presents Lester's voice from beyond the grave, rendering the rest of the film a flashback. "In less than a year, I'll be dead," says the voice-over, adding moments later, "I'm dead already." In a 2016 unpublished paper, Columbia University student Andrew Bell pointed out that the horizontal introduction of Jane—followed by Lester in bed—suggests "a shared apathy and sense of defeat. These characters are so beaten down by their environment, cultural expectation, and boredom that they're moribund. . . . All of Mendes' characters are trapped by the voyeuristic, judgmental gaze of the people around them."[2]

Accompanying a high-angle view of a suburban neighborhood, the repeated playful notes of Thomas Newman's score are like a musical analogue of the look-alike houses. As the film unfolds, it reveals what lies beneath the picture-perfect exterior. Misperception is key, especially when Fitts peers through Ricky's camera into Lester's house and sees his son close to their smiling neighbor. Although it looks like sex to the homophobic father, they are simply rolling a joint, which leads to a fatal denouement. The second sequence begins with Lester's reflection in the computer screen of his office, trapped behind bars of data. Like Jane in the opening, he is framed within a screen; unlike his daughter, he is alone, a mere copy of a human

FIGURE 8.2 Lester (Kevin Spacey) reflected in his computer in *American Beauty*

being. Despite the memorable red petals on Angela's body in fantasy scenes, *American Beauty* conveys the prick of the thorns under the rose.

The opening sequence is markedly different from Ball's early screenplay draft, which begins with Ricky in a jail cell. The second scene is in a courtroom, where Jane hears Angela testifying that Jane wanted her father dead. Fitts then brings evidence to the police station, including the footage of his son filming Jane. It is only on page 5 that the film as we know it begins. With the deletion of the more verbally dominated first four pages of the screenplay, *American Beauty* now opens with a video fragment that is visual, original, and disturbing.[3]

Lester's limbo is curiously related to that of another protagonist in a 1999 film, the unnamed narrator of *Fight Club* played by Edward Norton. The novel by Chuck Palahniuk, adapted by Joe Uhls and directed by David Fincher, gave rise to a fascinating, provocative, violent drama; it is often scathingly funny and ultimately requires a real leap of faith in psychological projection. Norton is superb in a role that seems derived from two of the previous showcases for his talent: as in *Primal Fear*, he has two different beings inside of him; as in *American History X*, he seems to be leading a cult of disenfranchised and aggressive young men but has a change of heart and tries to stop the violence. The voice-over takes us into his stream of consciousness from the beginning. In the vertiginous title sequence, Tyler (Brad Pitt) holds a gun in the mouth of Norton's character, three minutes before an explosion. We flash back to Norton in the arms of a burly guy (Meat Loaf) at a support group for men with testicular cancer. And after this opening, the film moves further back in time to Norton as a corporate worker with insomnia, addicted to support groups for cancer and TB, among other things, and able to sleep only after sobbing. When he meets

FIGURE 8.3 The superimpositions that introduce *Fight Club*

Tyler on an airplane, they decide to develop an underground fight club, where they and other guys exult in the primal appeal of crunch and blood. The end of the film returns to the first shot as Norton watches a corporate building explode. *Fight Club* culminates in his destroying symbols of what we owe to the twentieth century. Eerily prescient of the Twin Towers crumbling two years later, the closing (and opening) image depicts a destruction that is symbolic: because the financial institutions have records of debt, the characters let them crumble in order to start fresh. Like *A Clockwork Orange*, *Fight Club* is about fascism but cannot be called a fascist film.

American Beauty and *Fight Club* both reflect and question turn-of-the-millennium anxieties. In each, the protagonist begins as a weak, passive, and physically unassuming consumer. He has a meaningless office job and no sex life, while his spiritual void translates into physical recession. In the course of the film, he transforms himself: physical strength externalizes emotional power as he takes control of his life. Violence is cathartic, whether it is Lester hurling asparagus at the dining room wall or Norton pummeling a sparring partner. Both protagonists quit their jobs and blackmail their bosses. They become sexually potent, liberated by fantasy, which paradoxically awakens them to reality. Toward the end, both heroes have a moral awakening that is redemptive—Lester refusing the temptation of sex with an underage virgin, Norton abandoning the club. *American Beauty* and *Fight Club* have surprise endings: one answers the question of who killed Lester, and the other reveals the identity of Tyler. Although both films critique the stagnation of twentieth-century American life—especially consumerism—the endings diverge. Whereas Norton says, "Let it all fall," Lester embraces the beauty of the world.

The usual realms in which people find meaning—familial love, religion, art, and creative work—are voided in these movies. A sense of history or memory is absent, which is perhaps why Ricky feels he has to document everything. Lester is happy only when he looks at family photos of a good moment, and after he dies, he remembers the papery quality of his grandmother's skin. The dull heroes at the beginning of both films are like white bread waiting for something to be sandwiched in—or the buns of Smiley Burgers, where Lester ends up working. In the tradition of *Death of a Salesman*, they offer a quintessentially American dramatization of frustration, disappointment, and impotence. If *American Beauty* is about sleepwalking through personal history, *Fight Club* confronts sleepwalking through global history as well. Once both men let go of their moneymaking identities and embrace downward mobility, the possibility for transcendence appears. Ultimately, *American Beauty* and *Fight Club* deal with the deconstruction and reconstruction of our lives, reflecting unresolved tensions at the end of the twentieth century.

Many of the films in this book focus on male characters who are initially stuck, or suspended, and then activated into cinematic motion—externalized by images like the aquarium of

The Graduate, the wet windshield of *Taxi Driver*, the shower of *American Beauty*, and the drops of liquid that connect different time frames in *The Shipping News*. Whether looking through their eyes or engaging with characters via close-ups, we identify with the shaping of an identity. Unlike readers of a novel, we see the hero's evolution in a constant present tense: in *motion* pictures, identity is not finite but fluid. If the circular voice-over narration of 1940s thrillers implied inescapable fatality, the films of subsequent decades reflect an existentialist understanding: we are not necessarily born with an identity but create a self—freely and skeptically—through our choices and actions.

While the focus of most of the films in this book has been on male protagonists, the privileged narrative perspective is occasionally the domain of women. When characters address the camera in an opening scene, the result can be either intimate—as in Woody Allen's *Annie Hall* (1977)—or political, as in Warren Beatty's *Reds* (1981), but a voice that exists as a separate track creates a new layer of tension between what we see and hear. Terrence Malick's *Badlands* (1974) explores a female subjectivity, as the voice-over belongs to Holly (Sissy Spacek). (In *Days of Heaven* as well, Malick's addition of the voice-over of Linda Manz—who plays Richard Gere's sister—provides a crunchy counterpoint to the film's lacquered compositions.) In the first image of *Badlands*, Holly plays with her dog on a bed; as the camera moves back, her voice recalls her arrival in South Dakota with her father. The second part of the opening shows a garbage truck moving through bucolic suburban streets before we meet Kit (Martin Sheen). Finding a dead dog, this trash collector says to his buddy, "I'll give you a dollar if you eat this collie." Malick thus introduces both the off-kilter Kit and the repetition of animal images that gives the film poetic coherence. In the third part of the opening sequence, Holly twirls a baton outdoors while we hear her narration, "Little did I realize that what began in the alleys and back-ways of this quiet town would end in the badlands of Montana." Her singsong voice flattens the action, making us aware of the storytelling itself. And since she is narrating from a future point in time, we assume she will survive the tale of young killers on the run. More importantly, the subjectivity suggests that everything we see must be questioned. When Kit balances a broom vertically, he is visually connected to Holly and her baton, even before he notices her on the lawn.

While these elements depict an American landscape, Malick's style is markedly European: like François Truffaut and Jean-Luc Godard, he uses voice-over as a distancing device that renders the film a reverie. Loosely based on the murderous rampage of real-life teen couple Charles Starkweather and Caril Ann Fugate fifteen years earlier, it is a haunting hybrid of the road movie and gangster genres. Like *Bonnie and Clyde* (1967, for which Malick's wife served as an assistant), *Badlands* interrogates the mythologizing of the outlaw. Both Warren Beatty's Clyde and Sheen's Kit substitute violence for sex, aggressively creating their own legends (including a female sidekick). Kit makes a spoken record "for the D.A. to find"; later talks into a Dictaphone, offering platitudes to younger people; leaves objects in a pail to be found after he is gone; and finally marks a point in the path where his arrest takes place. His gestures are part of a self-conscious pattern, including wiping his fingerprints from a doorknob (after leaving them on everything else in the house they robbed). And before he is arrested, he checks his appearance in the rearview mirror of his car. Kit's resemblance to James Dean is literal and figurative, as he is obviously patterning his appearance on the movie star. The new names taken by

FIGURE 8.4 Martin Sheen and Sissy Spacek in the opening of *Badlands*

Kit and Holly are James and Priscilla (the latter perhaps invoking the wife of Elvis Presley). Even while robbing people, Kit is extremely polite, a paradoxical blend of minding manners and pointing guns.

From the opening sequence, Malick uses the music of Carl Orff to great contrapuntal effect. Beginning on xylophone, the score is enhanced by drums and—like a bolero—accumulates orchestration and texture. Its tinkling quality suggests a fairy tale, where innocence coexists with brutality. Often aestheticizing the action, the music heightens such images as a stereopticon, a raging fire, Kit and Holly moving down the river, a scarecrow, and a figure in the landscape reminiscent of the Crucifixion. We are also distanced visually—through the use of sepia footage, for instance, and when the camera fails to descend to a storm shelter to reveal the people Kit has shot. Rather, the film offers a progression of death through animals: after the dog left by the garbage truck, we see glimpses of dead fish, a cow, and finally Holly's father after Kit kills him. Malick singles out not only insects and a caged chicken but also airplane wheels and other images of movement. As the couple moves from the suburbs to the plains, they fulfill the line, "It's not what you say, but where you go." Substituting for the garbage truck of the opening, a stolen Cadillac becomes Kit's emblem of mobility: it presents space as interior landscape; that is, as emptiness.

The cadence of Spacek's voice-over feeds into Malick's devaluing of language. Like the curlers Holly wears, her tone is a product of romance magazines. Her line, "Each lived for the precious hours that he or she could be with the other," is followed by Holly saying on-screen, "My stomach's growling." Her name itself suggests Hollywood. If *Badlands* is structured by two narrators—the heroine's voice and the camera—they occasionally come into conflict. In films like *Days of Heaven* and *Tree of Life*, Malick would develop the use of contrapuntal voice-over; rather than being redundant with the images, it invites a meditation on them.

When movies present circular narration through voice-over or flashbacks, they lead us to question who we can trust: the narrator? unreliable; the director? manipulative. Can we believe our perceptions? No, they are too limited, especially when movies begin with the voice of someone who is dead. Misdirection is a strategy that prevents us from taking anything for granted, especially the manipulations of gifted filmmakers.

Whether exploring visual rhymes, voyeurism, space, or subjectivity, opening sequences guide us into the dynamic and meaningful unfolding of an on-screen narrative. As director Tom Tykwer acknowledged during a master class at the 2003 Berlin International Film Festival, a first scene "creates enormous intention, and attention for the audience."[4] We can add a third term: between the filmmakers' intent and the viewers' reception is the *tension* of anticipation. The audience has to be invested in what happens next. However, clips and photos can provide only a glimmer of that experience; we must watch the films in their entirety to appreciate how they create internal coherence and offer continuing resonance.

Let us end where we began. The definition of *overture* includes, "A proposal, something offered to consideration"—which is my hope for the reader of this book.[5] *Overture* is a suggestive word to describe what draws me to the films discussed here. First, it is a musical term, referring to the prelude of a performance: an overture contains fragments from the compositions that will be heard in the entire work. Second, it comes from *ouverture* in French, meaning "opening," rooted in the Latin word *apertura*. In turn, this leads to *aperture*, the diameter of the exposed part of a lens, referring to the apparatus that must be opened for light to enter the camera. Finally, an overture is philosophical: when we open a book, or when a film opens for us, it ideally engenders openness in us toward characters in situations far from our own. In the best of cases, this openness creates lucidity.

Notes

1. Victor Brombert, "Opening Signals in Narrative," *New Literary History* 11 (1979–80): 501.
2. Ibid., 494.
3. Eleanor Bergstein, "Commentaries," *Dirty Dancing*, directed by Emile Ardolino (New York: Lionsgate, 2009), DVD.
4. Jan-Christopher Horak, *Saul Bass: Anatomy of Film Design* (Lexington: University Press of Kentucky, 2014). See also Pat Kirkham, *Saul Bass: A Life in Film and Design* (London: Laurence King, 2011); and Andreas A. Timmer's doctoral dissertation, "Making the Ordinary Extraordinary: The Film-Related Work of Saul Bass" (Columbia University, 1999).
   A related article in *Slant Magazine* discusses the importance of *The Pink Panther* (1963):

> Cue Henry Mancini's immortal "Pink Panther Theme" (dead ant, dead ant.) Enter the Pink Panther, not the titular diamond with a small flaw shaped like an animal that the movie is actually about, but Friz Freleng's irrepressible creation, an animated panther that would frame the rest of the series and go on to have a cartoon career of his own, one that kept Freleng going after his years at Warner Brothers. This is the one that put cartoon credit sequences on the map. It's my tribute to all those cartoon titles that were in vogue in the 60's like *Bell, Book, and Candle* and *It's a Mad, Mad,*

Mad, Mad World, as well as retro-60's titles like the ones for Andrew Bergman's *Honeymoon in Vegas. The Pink Panther* rearranges names from anagrams. He purrs up against Capucine's name. He ogles Claudia Cardinale's name. He wears a monocle and smokes a cigarette from a holder. He gives himself credit where credit isn't due. He mocks and cajoles various technicians. He gets chased around by Inspector Clouseau (look up bumbling in the dictionary) and leaves pink paw prints everywhere. He entertains us while the names go flashing by. And all the while, Mancini's music keeps playing.

(*Slant Magazine*, "5 for the Day: Title Sequences," November 17, 2006, http://www.slantmagazine.com/house/article/5-for-the-day-title -sequences)

5. Susana Sevilla Aho, "Things Are Not What They Seem," video essay, 6:19, filmed fall 2013, uploaded January 26, 2015, https://vimeo .com/117864748. She made the video for the University of Connecticut's Digital Media and Design class "Broadcast Graphics and Title Sequences," taught by motion graphics designer Samantha Olschan.

6. Anthony Minghella and Tom Tykwer offered fascinating insights into adaptation in general, and opening sequences in particular, during a 2003 master class at the Berlin International Film Festival. Their remarks focused on *The English Patient* and *Heaven*, Tykwer's terrific drama of 2002 based on a screenplay by Krzysztof Kieślowski and Krzysztof Piesiewicz. "Interview to Tom Tykwer and Anthony Minghella," YouTube video, 1:25:09, Script Factory Masterclasses, Berlinale Talent Campus, Berlin International Film Festival, 2003, posted by "FanFresFilms," October 6, 2013, https://www.youtube.com/watch ?v=oGwmJyl_ZvE.

7. E. L. Doctorow, *Writers on Writing: Collected Essays from "The New York Times,"* introduction by John Darnton (New York: Times Books, 2001).

2. The Opening Translated from Literature

1. Millicent Marcus, *Filmmaking by the Book: Italian Cinema and Literary Adaptation* (Baltimore and London: Johns Hopkins University Press, 1993), x–xi.

2. All Bernardo Bertolucci quotations in this discussion are from the Walter Reade Theater event and come from my personal notes.
3. Part of my analysis of *The Tin Drum* overlaps with my essay "Reassessing *The Tin Drum*," liner notes, *The Tin Drum*, directed by Volker Schlöndorff (New York: Kino Lorber, 1999), DVD.
4. Carrière invoked Bruegel, the Flemish painter of peasantry, in the DVD commentary of the film. Jean-Claude Carrière, "Commentaries," *The Tin Drum*, directed by Volker Schlöndorff (1979; New York: Criterion, 2004), DVD.
5. These quotations are from my personal notes.
6. John Hughes, "*The Tin Drum*: Volker Schlöndorff's 'Dream of Childhood,'" *Film Quarterly* 34, no. 3 (Spring 1981): 5.
7. Jack Kroll, "Bang the Drum Loudly," *Newsweek*, April 21, 1980.
8. Part of my analysis of *The Unbearable Lightness of Being* appeared in my book *Philip Kaufman* (Chicago: University of Illinois Press, 2012).
9. Quotations from the NYU event, of which there are several in this chapter, come from my personal notes.
10. Milan Kundera, *The Unbearable Lightness of Being*, trans. Michael Henry Heim (New York: Harper Perennial, 1999), 3.
11. Victor Brombert, "Opening Signals in Narrative," *New Literary History* 11 (1979–80): 498.

3. Narrative Within the Frame

1. See André Bazin, *What Is Cinema?*, translated by Hugh Gray (Oakland: University of California Press, 2004). And for an excellent study of his work and influence, read Dudley Andrew's *André Bazin* (New York: Columbia University Press, 1990).
2. Murch wrote, "Much of my own work in its formative years was stylistically indebted to Welles, and specifically to 'Touch of Evil': the use of the illicitly tape-recorded conversation in 'The Conversation' (written and directed by Francis Coppola in 1974) is similar in many ways to the final reel of 'Touch of Evil'; and the use of source music to score 'American Graffiti' (written and directed by George Lucas in 1973) is similar to Welles's copious use of source music in 'Touch of Evil' (even, as I learned from his memo, down to the specific methods used in recording)." Walter Murch, "Restoring the Touch of Genius to a Classic," *New York Times*, September 13, 1998.

3. Narrative Within the Frame

3. Julie Salamon, review of *The Player*, *Wall Street Journal*, December 15, 1992.
4. "Werner Herzog Interviewed by Lawrence O'Toole," by Lawrence O'Toole, *Film Comment*, November/December 1979, 48.
5. Paraphrased from my personal notes.
6. Roger Ebert, "Aguirre, the Wrath of God," Rogerebert.com, April 4, 1999, http://www.rogerebert.com/reviews/great-movie-aguirre-the-wrath-of-god-1972
7. Columbia University student Alies Sluiter's unpublished paper of May 2016 offers a sensitive comparison of *The Piano* to *The Mission* (1986), whose protagonists both

    > use music to connect with people they meet in the new, colonised lands in which they find themselves. Notably, the main musical theme of both films is introduced as diegetic score via the protagonist playing an instrument. In *The Mission*, Father Gabriel (Jeremy Irons) sits on a rock and plays his oboe, to entice the indigenous Guarani to come out from the forest and meet him. In *The Piano*, Ada (Holly Hunter) pokes her hand through a hole in the shipping crate and plays the theme with one hand while she comforts her sleeping daughter Flora (Anna Paquin), with the other. Both films utilize the main character's performance of musical instruments to drive the action forward, although they approach it in different ways.

    She highlights how Ennio Morricone's score for *The Mission* "explores two cultures colliding, through his use of traditional baroque composition techniques and instrumentation . . . as well as traditional South American drums and flutes." Alies Sluiter, "How Does Music Function as a Narrative Device in Roland Joffe's *The Mision* and Jane Campion's *The Piano*?" (paper prepared for "Analysis of Film Language," taught by the author, Columbia University, May 2016).
8. Christina Chrisostomo, "The Musical Construction of Identity in *The Piano* and *The Mission*" (paper prepared for "Analysis of Film Language," taught by the author, Columbia University, May 2016).
9. This true story was also the subject of Ben Ross's short *3 Believers* in 1990, starring Elżbieta Czyżewska and Olek Krupa.
10. Annette Insdorf, "Oscar Nominee *In Darkness* Illuminates History and Heroism," *Huffington Post*, February 9, 2012, http://www.huffingtonpost.com/annette-insdorf/in-darkness-review_b_1258078.html.

11. Agnieszka Holland, interview with the author, *Telluride Film Watch*, September 2011. Composer Antoni Komasa-Łazarkiewicz recalled:

> After my first discussions with Agnieszka I realized that "In Darkness" is going to be the greatest challenge in my career as a composer of music for film. The theme and the approach to it made us all pose fundamental questions about the nature of music itself, the role of musical narrative in such a story, and the way it's supposed to correspond with the reality depicted in the picture. It was clear from the start that we will have to forget about the conventional approach to film scoring, where the music simply supports the emotional narrative, builds tension or suspense and gives a boost to the action. I remember, that after having seen the first edit of the film, Agnieszka and I were very close to the decision not to use any score at all. We were dealing with a material so delicate and yet so intense, that we had to look for a different, deeper level, on which music could constitute its own narrative. The film has a subtle metaphysical tension. It's a metaphysics without the presence of God, hidden from His eyes. The two worlds in which the film is happening, interact with each other, and the role of the music should be to build the bridges between them, transport emotions and impulses between the underworld and the reality above ground.
>
> (Antoni Komasa-Łazarkiewicz, press kit for *In Darkness*, directed by Agnieszka Holland [Sony Pictures Classics, 2011])

4. Narrative Between the Frames

1. "French Resistance: Costa Gavras," interview by Maya Jaggi, *Guardian*, April 3, 2009, http://www.theguardian.com/film/2009/apr/04/costa-gavras.

2. Marguerite Duras, *Hiroshima, mon amour*, screenplay, trans. Richard Seaver (New York: Grove, 1994).

3. Pablo Picasso, "An Interview," *Artists on Art from the XIV to the XX Century*, ed. Robert Goldwater and Marco Treves (New York: Pantheon, 1945), 417.

4. Robert Hughes, ed., *Film: Book 2. Films of Peace and War* (New York: Grove, 1962), 51.

5. *Midnight Cowboy* also utilized this kind of dislocating montage in 1969; screenwriter Waldo Salt suggested that these were not flashbacks, but "flashpresents." Syd Field, "The Use of Flashbacks in Movies," Writers Store, n.d., https://www.writersstore.com/the-use-of-flashbacks/.

6. Part of my analysis of *Schindler's List* appeared in my book *Indelible Shadows: Film and the Holocaust* (Cambridge: Cambridge University Press, 2003), copyright © 2003 Annette Insdorf. Reprinted with permission.

7. Part of my analysis of *Three Colors: Red* appeared in my book *Double Lives, Second Chances: The Cinema of Krzysztof Kieslowski* (Evanston: Northwestern University Press, 2013).

8. "Coloring the Message," *In Camera* (Autumn 1994): 1.

9. *Shine* was shot by Geoffrey Simpson, who was also the cinematographer of Vincent Ward's visually sumptuous *The Navigator: A Medieval Odyssey* (1988).

10. Scott Hicks, press kit for *Shine*, directed by Scott Hicks (New York: Fine Line Features, 1996).

11. Bruce Newman, "*Shine*: The Movie," *Los Angeles Times*, November 17, 1996, http://articles.latimes.com/1996-11-17/entertainment/ca-65409_1_david-helfgott.

5. Singular Point of View

1. See Robert Warshow, *The Immediate Experience: Movies, Comics, Theatre, and Other Aspects of Popular Culture* (Cambridge: Harvard University Press, 2002); and Leo Braudy, *The World in a Frame: What We See in Films*, 25th anniversary edition (1976; repr., Chicago: University of Chicago Press, 2002).

2. The Bertolucci paraphrase is from my notes. Jan Epstein's description of the 1990 Cannes symposium is online in *Urbancinefile*: "At the Cannes Film Festival this year, a two hour symposium was held, attended by some of cinema's best known filmmakers and critics: Bernardo Bertolucci, Roman Polanski, Andrzej Wajda, Jane Campion, John Boorman, Dennis Hopper, Theo Angelopoulos, Derek Malcolm, and Annette Insdorf, amongst others. The forum was intended as a colloquium between filmmakers and critics—often seen as adversaries." Jan Epstein, "46th Melbourne Film Festival," Urbancinefile.com, n.d., http://www.urbancinefile.com.au/home/view.asp?a=338&s=features.

3. Mike Nichols, "Commentaries," *The Graduate*, directed by Mike Nichols (New York: Criterion, 1999), DVD.

4. Joseph Gelmis, *The Film Director as Superstar* (Garden City, NY: Doubleday, 1970), 277.

5. James Sanders, *Celluloid Skyline: New York and the Movies* (New York: Knopf, 2001), 397. Pauline Kael famously praised *Taxi Driver* for its ending, in which Travis Bickle, a murderer, is hailed as a hero because the city is sicker than he is.

6. "Walter Murch in Conversation with Joy Katz," by Joy Katz, *Parnassus: Poetry in Review. The Movie Issue* 22 (1997): 124–153.

7. John Milius and Francis Ford Coppola, *Apocalypse Now Redux* (New York: Talk Miramax/Hyperion, 2001), vi–vii.

8. Joseph Conrad, *Heart of Darkness* (New York: Signet Classics, 1950), 65.

9. D. W. Griffith famously used the same music with the thunderous arrival of the Ku Klux Klan in *Birth of a Nation* (1915).

10. Michael Herr, *Dispatches* (New York: Avon, 1978), 3.

11. Rita Kempley, "Come and See," *Washington Post*, September 25, 1987.

12. Simon Kessler, discussion in "Analysis of Film Language," taught by the author, Columbia University, April 1, 2016.

13. Patrick Ford, discussion in "Analysis of Film Language," taught by the author, Columbia University, April 1, 2016.

14. Kurt Vonnegut, *Slaughterhouse-Five* (New York: Random House, 2015), 93–95.

15. Roger Ebert, "Come and See," Rogerebert.com, June 16, 2010, http://www.rogerebert.com/reviews/great-movie-come-and-see-1985.

16. Rachel Cooke, "Samuel Moaz: My Life at War and My Hopes for Peace," *Guardian*, May 1, 2010, http://www.theguardian.com/film/2010/may/02/israel-lebanon-samuel-maoz-tanks. Bracketed material in this quotation is from the source.

17. J. Hoberman, "An Israeli Tank Rolls North, Fumbling to War, in *Lebanon*," *Village Voice*, August 4, 2010, http://www.villagevoice.com/film/an-israeli-tank-rolls-north-fumbling-to-war-in-lebanon-6394221.

6. The Collective Protagonist

1. Annette Insdorf, "Team Players," *Washington Post*, January 14, 1996, https://www.washingtonpost.com/archive/lifestyle/style/1996

/01/14/team-players/db317334-b644-40bf-8c4e-89b2adafc966/?utm
_term=.6e48dfc5a285.

2. A. O. Scott, "An Israeli Tale of Mistrust, Without the Finger-Pointing,"
   New York Times, February 3, 2010.

3. Insdorf, "Team Players."

4. Ettore Scola, interview with the author, March 21, 1984, personal
   notes from audio tape.

5. Ibid.

6. Part of the analysis of *Day for Night* appeared in my book *François
   Truffaut*, revised and updated edition (Cambridge: Cambridge University Press, 1994), copyright © 1994 Annette Insdorf. Reprinted
   with permission.

7. *Postcards from the Edge* (1990), directed by Mike Nichols, shares with
   Day for Night the destabilizing strategy of opening with a scene from
   the film within the film. And *The Stunt Man* (1980), directed by Richard Rush, is a delightful elaboration on the theme of fabrication.

8. A. O. Scott, "A House Divided by Exasperation," *New York Times*,
   December 29, 2011, http://www.nytimes.com/2011/12/30/movies/a
   -separation-directed-by-asghar-farhadi-review.html.

9. A video entitled "Making of 'A Separation'" reveals that the camera
   was placed under the glass of a photocopy machine made especially
   for the shoot: https://www.youtube.com/watch?v=r5SCsMMFaCw.
   "Making of 'A Separation,'" YouTube video, 19:28, posted by "Man-
   sour Behabadi," November 23, 2012.

10. Anthony Lane, "Tehran Tales," *New Yorker*, January 9, 2012, http://
    www.newyorker.com/magazine/2012/01/09/tehran-tales.

11. Godfrey Cheshire, "Scenes from a Marriage," *Film Comment*, January/
    February 2012, http://www.filmcomment.com/article/scenes-from
    -a-marriage/.

12. Masoud Golsorkhi, "A Separation Can't Be Divorced from Iranian
    Politics," *Guardian*, July 5, 2011, http://www.theguardian.com/film/
    filmblog/2011/jul/05/a-separation-iranian-politics.

13. Anne Thompson, "Farhadi Talks Oscar Front-Runner A Separation;
    Divorce Drama Questions Iran's Future," *Indiewire*, December 30,
    2011, http://www.indiewire.com/2011/12/farhadi-talks-oscar-front-runner
    -a-separation-divorce-drama-questions-irans-future-183625/.

14. Nadine Labaki's previous feature *Caramel* (2008) is also an ensemble
    piece whose opening sequence establishes her thematic concerns
    and stylistic approach: to the strains of a tango (the score is again by

Khaled Mouzanar), the camera tracks above a creamy dark surface being cooked on a stove. After the bubbling liquid becomes rivulets, women joyfully place the sticky caramel in their mouths. The comedy then unfolds in a Beirut beauty salon (where the caramel is also used as a depilatory). Like a Lebanese Almodóvar, Labaki portrays wacky women with affection.

7. Misdirection/Visual Narration

1. Part of my analysis of *The Hourglass Sanatorium* appeared in my book *Intimations: The Cinema of Wojciech Has* (Chicago: Northwestern University Press), 2017.

2. *Oxford Dictionary of Quotations*, 5th edition, s.v. "Jean-Luc Godard."

3. Roger Ebert, "Before the Rain," Rogerebert.com, March 10, 1995, http://www.rogerebert.com/reviews/before-the-rain-1995.

4. Genesis 16:11–12 (King James Bible), http://biblehub.com/kjv/genesis /16.htm: "And the angel of the LORD said unto her, Behold, you art with child, and shalt bear a son, and shalt call his name Ishmael; because the LORD hath heard thy affliction. And he will be a wild man; his hand will be against every man, and every man's hand against him; and he shall dwell in the presence of all his brethren."

5. Bijan Tehrani, "A Conversation with Yaron Shani about making *Ajami*," *Cinema Without Borders*, January 13, 2010, http://cinemawith-outborders.com/conversations/2055-a-conversation-with-yaron-shani -about-making-of-ajami.html.

6. Kenneth Turan, "Review: 'Ajami,'" *Los Angeles Times*, February 19, 2010, http://articles.latimes.com/2010/feb/19/entertainment/la-et -ajami19-2010feb19.

7. Samuel Rimland, "Contemporary Conflict in Cinema: Comparative Approaches in *Ajami* and *Before the Rain*" (paper prepared for "Analysis of Film Language," taught by the author, Columbia University, April 2016).

8. Annette Insdorf, "Intervening Images: An Interview with Roger Spottiswoode," *Cinéaste* 13, no. 2 (1984): 39–40. One can compare this acknowledgment to that of Aleksander in *Before the Rain*, expressing guilt because his photographic intervention got someone killed.

9. Murch revealed that the actor Frederic Forrest placed the emphasis on *us* during one "wrong" take, which the editor added to the final mix. Walter Murch, "He'd Kill Us If He Had the Chance," Web of

Stories video, 03:33, n.d., https://www.webofstories.com/play/walter
.murch/64.

10. Part of my analysis of *Rising Sun* appeared in my book *Philip Kaufman* (Chicago: University of Illinois Press, 2012).

11. Annette Insdorf, *Philip Kaufman* (Champaign: University of Illinois Press, 2012), 2.

12. Leo Braudy, "Hitchcock, Truffaut, and the Irresponsible Audience," *Film Quarterly* 21, no. 4 (Summer 1968): 21–27.

13. David Thomson, "My Favourite Film: The Truman Show," *Guardian*, December 16, 2011, https://www.theguardian.com/film/filmblog/2011 /dec/16/my-favourite-film-truman-show.

8. Voice-Over Narration/Flashback

1. Victor Brombert, "Opening Signals in Narrative," *New Literary History* 11 (1979–80): 489–502.

2. Andrew Bell, "*American Beauty*: White Picket Prisons" (paper written for "Analysis of Film Language," taught by the author, Columbia University, May 8, 2016).

3. Alan Ball, "American Beauty" (unpublished draft, n.d.), http:// mypage.netlive.ch/demandit/files/M_BFNO38KLSZ567NYSJ29/ dms/modul_03/American_Beauty_early_draft.pdf.

4. "Interview to Tom Tykwer and Anthony Minghella," YouTube video, 1:25:09, Script Factory Masterclasses, Berlinale Talent Campus, Berlin International Film Festival, 2003, posted by "FanFresFilms," October 6, 2013, https://www.youtube.com/watch?v=oGwmJyl_ZvE.

5. *The New Encyclopaedia; or, Universal Dictionary of Arts and Sciences*, vol. 16 (London: Vernor, Hood, and Sharpe, 1807), s.v. "overture."

Index